Animal FACTS For Kids

Published by Willow Creek Press, Inc.
P.O. Box 147, Minocqua, Wisconsin 54548

Printed in the United States

Animal FACTS For Kids

FUN AND FASCINATING CREATURES FROM AROUND THE WORLD

WILLOW CREEK PRESS®

INTRODUCTION

WELCOME TO ANIMAL FACTS FOR KIDS! HAVE YOU EVER WONDERED WHY CHAMELEONS CHANGE COLOR, HOW FAST A CHEETAH CAN RUN, OR WHY WHALES SING? THIS BOOK IS YOUR TICKET TO A WILD ADVENTURE THROUGH THE AMAZING WORLD OF ANIMALS.

FROM THE TINY ANT TO THE MIGHTY ELEPHANT, EVERY CREATURE HAS ITS OWN INCREDIBLE STORY. IN THESE PAGES, YOU'LL MEET ANIMALS THAT CAN FLY, SWIM, JUMP, AND EVEN GLOW IN THE DARK! YOU'LL LEARN ABOUT THEIR SUPERPOWERS, QUIRKY BEHAVIORS, AND THE AMAZING WAYS THEY SURVIVE IN NATURE.

WHETHER YOU'RE A CURIOUS EXPLORER, AN ANIMAL LOVER, OR SOMEONE WHO JUST WANTS TO DISCOVER FUN FACTS, THIS BOOK IS PACKED WITH SURPRISES THAT WILL MAKE YOU SAY, "WOW!" GET READY TO EXPLORE JUNGLES, DIVE INTO OCEANS, TREK ACROSS DESERTS, AND CLIMB HIGH INTO THE MOUNTAINS – ALL WITHOUT LEAVING YOUR SEAT.

SO GRAB YOUR IMAGINATION AND LET'S DIVE INTO THE FASCINATING LIVES OF THE ANIMALS THAT SHARE OUR WORLD. WHO KNOWS? YOU MIGHT EVEN FIND A NEW FAVORITE ANIMAL ALONG THE WAY!

OWLS

NIGHTTIME HUNTERS

OWLS ARE NOCTURNAL, MEANING THEY'RE AWAKE AT NIGHT AND SLEEP DURING THE DAY. THEY USE THE DARK TO HUNT FOR FOOD!

Owls Around the World

THERE ARE ABOUT 250 DIFFERENT KINDS OF OWLS AROUND THE WORLD, FROM FORESTS AND DESERTS TO GRASSLANDS AND EVEN CITIES. THE ONLY PLACE YOU WON'T FIND THEM IS ANTARCTICA!

SUPER HEARING

OWLS CAN HEAR SOUNDS THAT ARE SUPER FAR AWAY, EVEN TINY SQUEAKS FROM A MOUSE UNDER THE SNOW.

NEST CHOICES

OWLS DON'T BUILD THEIR OWN NESTS. THEY USE TREE HOLES, ABANDONED NESTS, OR EVEN BARNS TO RAISE THEIR YOUNG.

NECK SPINNERS

OWLS CAN TURN THEIR HEADS ALMOST ALL THE WAY AROUND, ABOUT 270 DEGREES! THAT'S LIKE LOOKING OVER YOUR SHOULDER WITHOUT MOVING YOUR BODY.

Owls Hunting Owls

SOME OWLS HUNT OTHER OWLS! GREAT HORNED OWLS ARE THE BIGGEST PREDATORS OF THE SMALLER BARRED OWL.

HOOT, HOOT

NOT ALL OWLS HOOT! SOME SCREECH, WHISTLE, OR EVEN BARK TO COMMUNICATE WITH EACH OTHER.

Eye Colors Mean Something

OWLS WITH YELLOW EYES HUNT DURING THE DAY, ORANGE-EYED OWLS HUNT AT DUSK, AND DARK-EYED OWLS ARE NIGHT HUNTERS.

GROUNDHOGS

DIGGING MASTERS

GROUNDHOGS ARE AMAZING DIGGERS. THEY BUILD UNDERGROUND BURROWS WITH MULTIPLE ROOMS AND EXITS, INCLUDING SPECIAL AREAS FOR SLEEPING, STORING FOOD, AND EVEN A BATHROOM!

Forever Growing Teeth

THEIR FRONT TEETH NEVER STOP GROWING, SO GROUNDHOGS CHEW ON PLANTS TO KEEP THEM TRIMMED.

BEHIND THE NAME

GROUNDHOGS, ALSO CALLED WOODCHUCKS, GOT THEIR NAME FROM THE NATIVE AMERICAN WORD "WUCHAK."

DEEP SLEEP

GROUNDHOGS HIBERNATE DURING THE WINTER. THEY SLEEP FOR MONTHS IN THEIR BURROWS TO STAY WARM AND SAVE ENERGY UNTIL SPRING.

GRIZZLY BEARS

Protective and Territorial

GRIZZLIES ARE GENERALLY SOLITARY ANIMALS, AND THEY CAN BE VERY PROTECTIVE OF THEIR TERRITORY AND FOOD, ESPECIALLY DURING LATE SUMMER AND EARLY FALL.

BIG AND STRONG

GRIZZLY BEARS ARE HUGE! THEY CAN WEIGH UP TO 800 POUNDS AND STAND OVER 7 FEET TALL ON THEIR HIND LEGS.

A BALANCED DIET

GRIZZLY BEARS EAT BOTH PLANTS AND ANIMALS. THEIR DIET INCLUDES BERRIES, ROOTS, FISH, INSECTS, AND SMALL MAMMALS.

Hibernation Experts

GRIZZLY BEARS HIBERNATE DURING THE WINTER. THEY SLEEP IN DENS FOR MONTHS, SURVIVING ON STORED FAT TO STAY WARM AND ENERGIZED.

JAGUARS

Beautiful Spots

JAGUARS HAVE GOLDEN-YELLOW FUR WITH BLACK SPOTS CALLED ROSETTES. EACH JAGUAR HAS A UNIQUE PATTERN, JUST LIKE FINGERPRINTS!

ENDANGERED SPECIES

JAGUARS ARE ENDANGERED DUE TO HABITAT LOSS AND POACHING. CONSERVATION EFFORTS ARE HELPING TO PROTECT THESE MAGNIFICENT ANIMALS AND THEIR HOMES.

Amazing Swimmers

UNLIKE MANY BIG CATS, JAGUARS LOVE WATER. THEY ARE EXCELLENT SWIMMERS AND OFTEN HUNT IN RIVERS AND LAKES.

SILENT HUNTERS

JAGUARS ARE SKILLED HUNTERS. THEY STALK THEIR PREY QUIETLY AND THEN POUNCE WITH INCREDIBLE SPEED AND STRENGTH.

LADYBUGS

PLAYING DEAD

IF A LADYBUG FEELS THREATENED, IT CAN PLAY DEAD BY CURLING UP AND STAYING STILL. SOMETIMES, IT EVEN RELEASES A BAD-SMELLING LIQUID TO SCARE OFF PREDATORS!

COLORFUL COATS

MOST LADYBUGS ARE RED OR ORANGE WITH BLACK SPOTS, BUT SOME CAN BE YELLOW, PINK, OR EVEN BLACK WITH DIFFERENT PATTERNS.

Symbol of Luck

IN MANY CULTURES, LADYBUGS ARE SEEN AS A SIGN OF GOOD LUCK AND ARE BELIEVED TO BRING HAPPINESS AND PROSPERITY.

GARDEN HELPERS

LADYBUGS LOVE TO EAT PESTS LIKE APHIDS, WHICH HARM PLANTS. THAT'S WHY GARDENERS AND FARMERS LOVE HAVING THEM AROUND.

LEMURS

NIGHT VISION

MANY LEMURS HAVE LARGE, BRIGHT EYES THAT HELP THEM SEE WELL IN THE DARK, AS SOME ARE NOCTURNAL.

MADAGASCAR NATIVES

LEMURS ARE ONLY FOUND IN THE WILD ON THE ISLAND OF MADAGASCAR AND A FEW NEARBY ISLANDS— NOWHERE ELSE IN THE WORLD!

TAILS THAT TALK

RING-TAILED LEMURS HAVE LONG, STRIPED TAILS WITH BLACK AND WHITE RINGS. THEY USE THEIR TAILS FOR BALANCE AND TO COMMUNICATE WITH THEIR GROUP.

OLDEST LIVING PRIMATES

LEMURS ARE AMONG THE OLDEST PRIMATES IN THE WORLD, WITH ANCESTORS DATING BACK ABOUT 60 MILLION YEARS!

BEES

BUZZING FOR HONEY

BEES COLLECT NECTAR FROM FLOWERS AND TURN IT INTO HONEY, WHICH THEY USE AS FOOD DURING WINTER.

Busy Pollinators

BEES HELP POLLINATE PLANTS, WHICH MEANS THEY MOVE POLLEN FROM FLOWER TO FLOWER, HELPING FRUITS, VEGETABLES, AND FLOWERS GROW.

A COLORFUL CAST

THERE ARE OVER 20,000 BEE SPECIES THAT COME IN ALL SHAPES, SIZES, AND COLORS, FROM TINY SWEAT BEES TO LARGE BUMBLEBEES.

TO STING OR NOT TO STING

ONLY FEMALE BEES CAN STING, AND SOME SPECIES, DON'T HAVE STINGERS AT ALL.

MOOSE

Standing Tall

MOOSE ARE THE LARGEST MEMBERS OF THE DEER FAMILY. ADULT MALES, CALLED BULLS, CAN WEIGH UP TO 1,500 POUNDS AND STAND SIX FEET TALL AT THE SHOULDER!

LEG DAY CHAMPS

MOOSE HAVE LONG LEGS THAT HELP THEM WALK THROUGH DEEP SNOW AND WETLANDS. THEIR LONG LEGS ALSO HELP THEM REACH FOOD IN TALL TREES.

Listen Up

MOOSE HAVE BIG, FLOPPY EARS THAT HELP THEM HEAR PREDATORS AND COMMUNICATE WITH OTHER MOOSE. THEIR EARS ALSO HELP THEM STAY COOL IN HOT WEATHER.

SOLITARY CREATURES

MOOSE ARE SOLITARY ANIMALS, MEANING THEY PREFER TO LIVE ALONE, EXCEPT DURING MATING SEASON OR WHEN A MOTHER IS RAISING HER CALF.

CHAMELEONS

Color-Changing Wizards

CHAMELEONS ARE FAMOUS FOR CHANGING COLOR! THEY DO THIS TO COMMUNICATE, SHOW EMOTION, OR ADJUST TO TEMPERATURE, NOT JUST TO CAMOUFLAGE.

CURLY TAILS

CHAMELEONS HAVE PREHENSILE TAILS, WHICH MEANS THEY CAN USE THEIR TAILS TO GRAB ONTO BRANCHES, JUST LIKE A FIFTH LIMB.

Tongue Superheroes

A CHAMELEON'S TONGUE CAN BE TWICE AS LONG AS ITS BODY. THEY USE IT TO CATCH INSECTS IN THE BLINK OF AN EYE!

A WORLD OF CHAMELEONS

THERE ARE MORE THAN 200 SPECIES OF CHAMELEONS, AND MOST OF THEM LIVE IN AFRICA AND MADAGASCAR.

SQUIRRELS

WEATHER PREDICTORS

IN WINTER, SQUIRRELS GROW THICKER FUR TO STAY WARM. THEY'RE LIKE LITTLE WEATHER FORECASTERS FOR THE COLD!

Worldwide Family

THERE ARE ABOUT 285 SPECIES OF SQUIRRELS, FOUND ALMOST EVERYWHERE IN THE WORLD EXCEPT ANTARCTICA AND AUSTRALIA!

NUTTY HIDERS

SQUIRRELS HIDE THOUSANDS OF NUTS EVERY YEAR, BUT THEY DON'T REMEMBER ALL THEIR HIDING SPOTS. SOME GROW INTO TREES!

FLYING GLIDERS

FLYING SQUIRRELS DON'T ACTUALLY FLY. THEY GLIDE THROUGH THE AIR USING SPECIAL FLAPS OF SKIN.

ACORN EXPERTS

SOME SQUIRRELS CAN TELL IF AN ACORN IS ROTTEN JUST BY SHAKING IT OR SMELLING IT.

Fearless Fallers

SQUIRRELS CAN FALL FROM INCREDIBLE HEIGHTS WITHOUT GETTING HURT! THEIR LIGHTWEIGHT BODIES, BUSHY TAILS, AND STRONG LEGS HELP THEM LAND SAFELY EVERY TIME.

ZIGZAG RUNNERS

WHEN SQUIRRELS FEEL THREATENED, THEY RUN AWAY IN A ZIGZAG PATTERN. THIS IS AN INCREDIBLY USEFUL STRATEGY TO ESCAPE HAWKS AND OTHER PREDATORS.

Squirrel Teeth Never Stop Growing

LIKE BEAVERS, SQUIRREL TEETH GROW CONTINUOUSLY AND STAY SHARP FROM ALL THEIR CHEWING.

POLAR BEARS

BUILT FOR THE COLD

POLAR BEARS HAVE A THICK LAYER OF FUR AND FAT THAT KEEPS THEM WARM IN FREEZING TEMPERATURES. THEIR FUR IS ACTUALLY TRANSLUCENT, BUT IT LOOKS WHITE BECAUSE IT REFLECTS LIGHT.

Kings of the Arctic

POLAR BEARS ARE THE LARGEST LAND CARNIVORES! ADULT MALES CAN WEIGH UP TO 1,500 POUNDS AND GROW AS LONG AS 10 FEET, INCLUDING THEIR TAIL.

SEA BEARS

POLAR BEARS ARE EXCELLENT SWIMMERS! THEY CAN SWIM FOR MILES IN ICY COLD WATERS, USING THEIR LARGE PAWS LIKE PADDLES.

THE NOSE KNOWS

POLAR BEARS HAVE AN INCREDIBLE SENSE OF SMELL. THEY CAN DETECT A SEAL'S SCENT FROM MILES AWAY AND CAN SNIFF OUT PREY THROUGH THICK LAYERS OF ICE.

QUOKKAS

Furry Friends

QUOKKAS ARE SMALL, KANGAROO-LIKE MARSUPIALS, ABOUT THE SIZE OF A DOMESTIC CAT. THEY HAVE ROUND FACES AND FLUFFY FUR, MAKING THEM LOOK VERY CUDDLY.

THE HAPPIEST ANIMAL

QUOKKAS ARE OFTEN CALLED "THE HAPPIEST ANIMALS IN THE WORLD" BECAUSE THEY HAVE A FRIENDLY, SMILING EXPRESSION ON THEIR FACES THAT MAKES THEM LOOK LIKE THEY'RE ALWAYS HAPPY!

AUSTRALIAN ORIGINAL

QUOKKAS ARE FOUND ONLY IN THE WILD ON A FEW SMALL ISLANDS OFF THE COAST OF WESTERN AUSTRALIA, LIKE ROTTNEST ISLAND. THEY ALSO LIVE IN SOME FORESTED AREAS OF THE MAINLAND.

Hydration Hackers

QUOKKAS CAN GO FOR LONG PERIODS WITHOUT DRINKING WATER. THEY GET MOST OF THE MOISTURE THEY NEED FROM THE PLANTS THEY EAT.

PORCUPINES

Prickly Yet Perfect

PORCUPINES ARE COVERED IN SHARP QUILLS THAT PROTECT THEM FROM PREDATORS. THESE QUILLS ARE LIKE NEEDLES AND ARE VERY DIFFICULT TO REMOVE ONCE THEY STICK INTO SOMETHING.

NO DRAMA, JUST QUILLS

PORCUPINES ARE NOT AGGRESSIVE ANIMALS. THEY PREFER TO STAY QUIET AND PEACEFUL, ONLY USING THEIR QUILLS FOR DEFENSE WHEN THEY FEEL THREATENED.

Easy Does It

PORCUPINES ARE SLOW-MOVING CREATURES. THEY TEND TO TAKE THEIR TIME WHILE WALKING AROUND, BUT THEY CAN CLIMB AND MOVE QUICKLY WHEN NEEDED.

ODOR ALERT

IF THREATENED, PORCUPINES CAN RELEASE A FOUL-SMELLING LIQUID FROM THEIR GLANDS TO WARN PREDATORS TO STAY AWAY.

PRAYING MANTISES

MATING DANCE

MALE PRAYING MANTISES OFTEN PERFORM A "DANCE" TO ATTRACT FEMALES. BUT SOMETIMES, THE FEMALE MIGHT EAT THE MALE AFTER MATING!

HOLY HUNTERS

THEY GET THEIR NAME FROM THE WAY THEY HOLD THEIR FRONT LEGS, WHICH LOOK LIKE THEY'RE IN A PRAYING POSITION. BUT THEY'RE ACTUALLY READY TO CATCH PREY!

FAST REFLEXES

PRAYING MANTISES HAVE LIGHTNING-FAST REFLEXES. WHEN THEY CATCH PREY, THEY CAN STRIKE IN A SPLIT SECOND, USING THEIR POWERFUL FORELEGS.

Eyes Everywhere

PRAYING MANTISES HAVE VERY LARGE EYES THAT ALLOW THEM TO SEE NEARLY 360 DEGREES AROUND THEM. THIS HELPS THEM SPOT PREY FROM A DISTANCE.

SLOTHS

Fur with a Purpose

SLOTHS HAVE A SPECIAL GREENISH TINGE TO THEIR FUR, WHICH COMES FROM ALGAE GROWING IN IT. THIS HELPS THEM BLEND INTO THE TREES AND STAY HIDDEN FROM PREDATORS.

TREE DWELLERS

SLOTHS LIVE IN THE RAINFOREST AND SPEND ALMOST THEIR ENTIRE LIVES HANGING UPSIDE DOWN IN TREES. THEY USE THEIR LONG CLAWS TO GRIP BRANCHES TIGHTLY.

Speed Isn't Everything

SLOTHS ARE FAMOUS FOR BEING EXTREMELY SLOW. THEY MOVE AT A PACE OF ABOUT 0.03 MILES PER HOUR, MAKING THEM ONE OF THE SLOWEST ANIMALS ON EARTH!

TOE-TALLY UNIQUE

THERE ARE TWO TYPES OF SLOTHS: THREE-TOED AND TWO-TOED. DESPITE THE NAMES, BOTH TYPES HAVE THREE TOES ON THEIR BACK FEET, BUT THE FRONT FEET ARE DIFFERENT!

RED PANDAS

Himalayan Huggers

RED PANDAS LIVE IN THE MOUNTAINOUS FORESTS OF THE HIMALAYAS AND PARTS OF CHINA, WHERE IT'S COOL AND MISTY.

FLUFFY AND FABULOUS

RED PANDAS ARE SMALL AND ADORABLE, WEIGHING ABOUT AS MUCH AS A HOUSE CAT. THEY HAVE FLUFFY TAILS AND RED-BROWN FUR THAT HELPS KEEP THEM WARM IN THEIR COLD MOUNTAIN HABITATS.

More Raccoon Than Panda

EVEN THOUGH THEY'RE CALLED RED PANDAS, THEY'RE NOT CLOSELY RELATED TO GIANT PANDAS! THEY'RE MORE CLOSELY RELATED TO RACCOONS AND WEASELS.

ONE'S COMPANY

RED PANDAS ARE MOSTLY SOLITARY ANIMALS. THEY LIKE TO BE ALONE AND COMMUNICATE WITH EACH OTHER THROUGH SCENT MARKINGS AND CALLS.

SPIDERS

Not All Spin Webs

WHILE MANY SPIDERS SPIN WEBS TO CATCH FOOD, SOME, LIKE JUMPING SPIDERS, CHASE DOWN THEIR PREY INSTEAD!

WATER WALKERS

SOME SPIDERS, LIKE FISHING SPIDERS, CAN WALK ON WATER AND EVEN DIVE TO CATCH FISH OR TADPOLES.

SPIDER SILK FOR SAFETY

SPIDERS USE SILK NOT JUST FOR WEBS BUT ALSO TO MAKE SAFETY LINES WHEN CLIMBING OR TO PROTECT THEIR EGGS.

MOSTLY HARMLESS

ONLY A FEW SPIDERS, LIKE BLACK WIDOWS AND BROWN RECLUSES, HAVE VENOM STRONG ENOUGH TO HURT HUMANS. MOST SPIDERS ARE HARMLESS.

Eight-Legged Wonders

ALL SPIDERS HAVE EIGHT LEGS, WHICH HELP THEM MOVE QUICKLY AND CLIMB ALMOST ANYWHERE.

TOCO TOUCANS

GREAT CLIMBERS

TOCO TOUCANS ARE EXCELLENT CLIMBERS! THEY USE THEIR STRONG FEET TO GRAB ONTO TREE BRANCHES AND MOVE AROUND IN THE DENSE RAINFORESTS OF SOUTH AMERICA.

Big Beak, No Burden

ALTHOUGH THEIR BEAKS ARE LARGE AND HEAVY-LOOKING, TOCO TOUCANS' BEAKS ARE ACTUALLY LIGHT, MADE FROM A HONEYCOMB STRUCTURE INSIDE THAT KEEPS THEM EASY TO CARRY AROUND.

COLORFUL BEAK

THE TOCO TOUCAN IS FAMOUS FOR ITS LARGE, COLORFUL BEAK, WHICH IS MOSTLY ORANGE WITH A BLACK TIP. THEIR BEAK CAN BE UP TO EIGHT INCHES LONG!

TREETOP TREATS

TOCO TOUCANS MOSTLY EAT FRUIT, LIKE BERRIES, BANANAS, AND SEEDS. THEY ALSO ENJOY EATING INSECTS, SMALL REPTILES, AND EGGS.

GOATS

BEARDED BEAUTIES

BOTH MALE AND FEMALE GOATS CAN HAVE BEARDS, WHICH ADD TO THEIR QUIRKY, CHARMING LOOKS.

Jumping with Joy

GOATS LOVE TO JUMP AND PLAY. BABY GOATS, CALLED KIDS, ESPECIALLY ENJOY HOPPING AROUND AND PRACTICING THEIR BALANCE.

BREEDS GALORE

THERE ARE OVER 200 DIFFERENT BREEDS OF GOATS, FROM TINY PYGMY GOATS TO LARGE BOER GOATS. EACH BREED HAS ITS OWN UNIQUE TRAITS.

WATER AVOIDERS

GOATS AREN'T FANS OF GETTING WET! THEY'LL LEAP OVER STREAMS AND PUDDLES WHENEVER THEY CAN TO KEEP THEIR HOOVES DRY.

SNEEZE ALERTS

GOATS USE SNEEZING AS THEIR BUILT-IN ALARM SYSTEM! A SNEEZE WARNS THE HERD OF DANGER.

CLIMBING CHAMPS

GOATS ARE AMAZING CLIMBERS! THEY CAN CLIMB STEEP HILLS, ROCKY CLIFFS, AND EVEN TREES TO FIND FOOD.

Rectangle Eyes

GOATS HAVE UNIQUE RECTANGULAR PUPILS THAT GIVE THEM A WIDE FIELD OF VISION, HELPING THEM SPOT DANGER FROM ALMOST ANY DIRECTION!

WILD BOARS

Built for the Wild

WILD BOARS ARE STRONG ANIMALS WITH POWERFUL BODIES. THEY HAVE THICK SKIN AND SHARP TUSKS THAT HELP THEM PROTECT THEMSELVES AND DIG FOR FOOD.

FAMILY FIRST

WILD BOARS LIVE IN GROUPS CALLED SOUNDERS. THESE GROUPS CAN INCLUDE UP TO 20 BOARS, LED BY A DOMINANT FEMALE. THE SOUNDER INCLUDES MOTHERS AND THEIR YOUNG BOARS.

SNOUT SCOUTS

WILD BOARS HAVE AN EXCELLENT SENSE OF SMELL, WHICH HELPS THEM FIND FOOD. THEY CAN SNIFF OUT BURIED ROOTS AND INSECTS IN THE SOIL, AND THEY USE THEIR SNOUT TO DIG THEM UP.

FOREST FOODIES

WILD BOARS ARE OMNIVORES, MEANING THEY EAT BOTH PLANTS AND ANIMALS. THEY ENJOY EATING ROOTS, FRUITS, NUTS, AND SMALL ANIMALS LIKE INSECTS, RODENTS, AND EVEN BIRDS.

ANTS

SUPER STRONG

ANTS CAN CARRY OBJECTS 50 TIMES THEIR OWN WEIGHT! THAT'S LIKE YOU LIFTING A CAR.

A World Full of Ants

THERE ARE OVER 12,000 SPECIES OF ANTS AROUND THE WORLD, AND MORE ARE DISCOVERED EVERY YEAR.

QUEENS RULE

THE QUEEN ANT LAYS ALL THE EGGS IN THE COLONY, MAKING HER THE MOTHER OF EVERY ANT IN THE NEST. SOME QUEENS CAN LAY THOUSANDS OF EGGS IN A SINGLE DAY, ENSURING THE COLONY GROWS AND THRIVES WITH PLENTY OF NEW WORKERS!

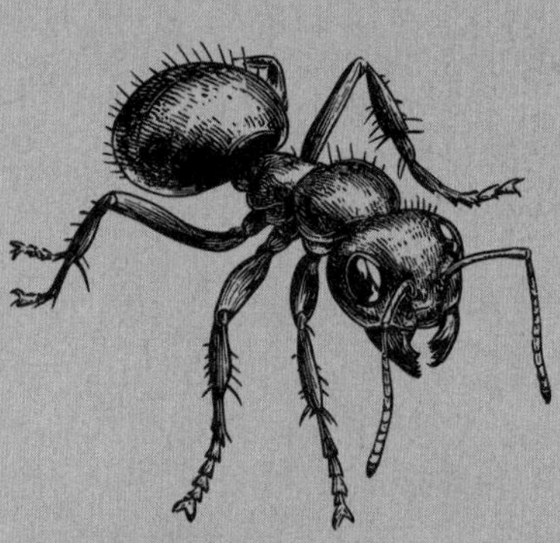

Ants Never Sleep

ANTS DON'T SLEEP LIKE HUMANS DO. THEY TAKE TINY NAPS THROUGHOUT THE DAY AND NIGHT. THESE QUICK REST BREAKS KEEP THEM ENERGIZED, ALLOWING THEM TO STAY ACTIVE AND HARDWORKING MOST OF THE TIME!

DONKEYS

SMALL BUT MIGHTY

DONKEYS ARE KNOWN FOR THEIR STRENGTH AND ENDURANCE. THEY MAY BE SMALLER THAN HORSES, BUT THEY ARE INCREDIBLY STRONG AND CAN CARRY HEAVY LOADS OVER LONG DISTANCES.

HEAR ME OUT

DONKEYS HAVE LARGE, LONG EARS THAT HELP THEM HEAR WELL. THEY CAN DETECT SOUNDS FROM FAR AWAY, WHICH HELPS THEM STAY ALERT TO ANY DANGERS.

MEMORY MASTERS

DONKEYS HAVE AN EXCELLENT MEMORY. THEY CAN REMEMBER PLACES, PEOPLE, AND OTHER ANIMALS FOR A LONG TIME, AND THEY TEND TO STICK TO ROUTINES.

LOUD AND PROUD

DONKEYS ARE KNOWN FOR THEIR LOUD BRAYING CALLS, WHICH THEY USE TO COMMUNICATE WITH EACH OTHER. THEIR CALLS CAN BE HEARD FROM A LONG DISTANCE.

KOALAS

EARS TO HEAR

KOALAS HAVE LARGE, ROUND EARS THAT HELP THEM HEAR WELL, EVEN IN THE DENSE FORESTS WHERE THEY LIVE. THEIR HEARING HELPS THEM DETECT PREDATORS OR CALLS FROM OTHER KOALAS.

Living the Dry Life

THE WORD "KOALA" COMES FROM THE ABORIGINAL LANGUAGE DHARUG AND MEANS "NO DRINK." THIS IS BECAUSE KOALAS GET MOST OF THEIR WATER FROM EUCALYPTUS LEAVES AND RARELY DRINK WATER IN THE WILD.

TREE-HUGGERS

KOALAS SPEND MOST OF THEIR LIVES IN TREES. THEY LIVE IN EUCALYPTUS FORESTS, WHERE THEY SLEEP IN THE BRANCHES FOR UP TO 20 HOURS A DAY!

NOT YOUR AVERAGE BEAR

KOALAS ARE OFTEN CALLED "KOALA BEARS," BUT THEY AREN'T ACTUALLY BEARS! THEY ARE MARSUPIALS, LIKE KANGAROOS AND WOMBATS, AND ARE MORE CLOSELY RELATED TO WOMBATS THAN BEARS.

RACCOONS

MASKED BANDITS

RACCOONS ARE KNOWN FOR THE "MASK" OF BLACK FUR AROUND THEIR EYES, WHICH MAKES THEM LOOK LIKE LITTLE BANDITS. THIS HELPS THEM BLEND INTO THE NIGHT WHILE THEY SEARCH FOR FOOD.

Tiny Hands, Big Skills

RACCOONS HAVE INCREDIBLY DEXTEROUS FRONT PAWS, WHICH THEY USE LIKE HANDS. THEY CAN GRAB, HOLD, AND MANIPULATE OBJECTS, AND THEY ARE OFTEN SEEN "WASHING" THEIR FOOD IN WATER, THOUGH THEY DON'T ACTUALLY NEED TO WASH IT.

SNEAKY AND SMART

RACCOONS ARE SUPER SMART! THEY ARE KNOWN FOR THEIR PROBLEM-SOLVING ABILITIES, AND THEY CAN OPEN LOCKS, LATCHES, AND EVEN DOORS TO GET TO FOOD.

SNIFF, HEAR AND FEEL

RACCOONS HAVE A KEEN SENSE OF HEARING AND SMELL, WHICH HELP THEM FIND FOOD IN THE DARK. THEIR SENSE OF TOUCH IS ALSO VERY SENSITIVE, ESPECIALLY IN THEIR PAWS.

ARMADILLOS

Rolling to Safety

SOME ARMADILLOS, LIKE THE THREE-BANDED ARMADILLO, CAN ROLL UP INTO A TIGHT BALL TO PROTECT THEIR SOFT UNDERSIDE FROM DANGER.

SUPER SWIMMERS

EVEN THOUGH THEY HAVE HEAVY SHELLS, ARMADILLOS ARE GREAT SWIMMERS. THEY CAN HOLD THEIR BREATH FOR UP TO SIX MINUTES AND EVEN WALK UNDERWATER!

ARMOR UP

ARMADILLOS ARE COVERED IN HARD, PROTECTIVE SHELLS MADE OF BONY PLATES, WHICH HELP KEEP THEM SAFE FROM PREDATORS.

Dig, Scoop, Feast

ARMADILLOS LOVE TO EAT BUGS, ESPECIALLY ANTS AND TERMITES. THEY USE THEIR SHARP CLAWS TO DIG AND THEIR LONG, STICKY TONGUES TO SCOOP UP THEIR MEALS.

WOLVES

Echoes of the Wild

WOLVES ARE FAMOUS FOR THEIR HOWLS, WHICH THEY USE TO COMMUNICATE WITH THEIR PACK. THEIR HOWLS CAN BE HEARD UP TO TEN MILES AWAY!

PACK RULES

WOLVES LIVE IN FAMILY GROUPS CALLED PACKS, USUALLY LED BY AN ALPHA PAIR (A MALE AND A FEMALE) WHO GUIDE AND PROTECT THE PACK.

Strength in Numbers

WHEN HUNTING, WOLVES USE TEAMWORK. THEY WORK TOGETHER TO CHASE AND CORNER PREY LIKE DEER OR ELK, USING STRATEGY AND COOPERATION.

FAST RUNNERS

WOLVES ARE GREAT RUNNERS AND CAN SPRINT UP TO 38 MILES PER HOUR TO CHASE PREY, THOUGH THEY USUALLY TRAVEL AT A SLOWER PACE.

PEACOCKS

Colorful Feathers

PEACOCKS ARE FAMOUS FOR THEIR VIBRANT, COLORFUL FEATHERS. THE MALE PEACOCK HAS A SPECTACULAR TAIL, CALLED A "TRAIN," COVERED IN BRIGHT BLUE, GREEN, AND GOLD FEATHERS THAT HE CAN FAN OUT IN A STUNNING DISPLAY.

BRIGHT AND BOLD

PEACOCKS FAN OUT THEIR TAIL FEATHERS TO ATTRACT FEMALES, SHOWING OFF THE BEAUTIFUL EYE-LIKE PATTERNS ON THE FEATHERS. THE LARGER AND MORE COLORFUL THE DISPLAY, THE MORE IMPRESSIVE IT IS TO POTENTIAL MATES.

BIG BIRDS

PEACOCKS ARE LARGE BIRDS. THE MALES CAN GROW UP TO SIX FEET LONG, INCLUDING THEIR TAIL FEATHERS, AND THEY WEIGH ABOUT 8–13 POUNDS.

Royalty in Feathers

IN MANY CULTURES, THE PEACOCK IS A SYMBOL OF BEAUTY, GRACE, AND PRIDE. ITS COLORFUL FEATHERS ARE OFTEN ASSOCIATED WITH ROYALTY AND ELEGANCE, AND IT'S EVEN THE NATIONAL BIRD OF INDIA.

FROGS

NO TAIL, NO PROBLEM

FROGS DON'T HAVE TAILS AS ADULTS, BUT THEY DO WHEN THEY'RE TADPOLES! THEY LOSE THEIR TAILS AS THEY GROW.

Big and Tiny

FROGS COME IN ALL SIZES. THE GOLIATH FROG IS AS BIG AS A CAT, WHILE THE TINY PAEDOPHRYNE FROG IS SMALLER THAN A DIME.

WORLD TRAVELERS

FROGS LIVE ON EVERY CONTINENT EXCEPT ANTARCTICA. YOU CAN FIND THEM IN FORESTS, DESERTS, AND EVEN YOUR BACKYARD!

SLIMY SKIN

A FROG'S SKIN IS SPECIAL BECAUSE IT HELPS THEM BREATHE AND STAY HYDRATED. THAT IS WHY FROGS NEED TO LIVE NEAR WATER.

POISON POWER

SOME FROGS, LIKE POISON DART FROGS, HAVE BRIGHT COLORS TO WARN PREDATORS THAT THEY'RE TOXIC AND NOT SAFE TO EAT.

Chorus Singers

FROGS ARE FAMOUS FOR THEIR CROAKS AND RIBBITS. MALE FROGS SING TO ATTRACT A MATE OR MARK THEIR TERRITORY.

FROG OR TOAD

ALL TOADS ARE FROGS, BUT NOT ALL FROGS ARE TOADS. TOADS USUALLY HAVE DRY, BUMPY SKIN, WHILE FROGS HAVE SMOOTH, SLIMY SKIN.

Amazing Color Changers

SOME FROGS CAN CHANGE COLORS TO BLEND INTO THEIR SURROUNDINGS, LIKE NATURE'S LITTLE CHAMELEONS!

ALBATROSSES

Flying the Extra Mile

ALBATROSSES ARE KNOWN FOR THEIR AMAZING ABILITY TO FLY LONG DISTANCES. THEY CAN FLY ACROSS ENTIRE OCEANS WITHOUT FLAPPING THEIR WINGS MUCH, USING WIND CURRENTS TO GLIDE EFFORTLESSLY.

WINGED GIANTS

ALBATROSSES ARE SOME OF THE LARGEST FLYING BIRDS IN THE WORLD. THEIR WINGSPAN CAN REACH UP TO 12 FEET, WHICH IS LONGER THAN A GROWN-UP IS TALL!

Love for Life

ALBATROSSES ARE KNOWN FOR THEIR STRONG BONDS WITH THEIR MATES. THEY OFTEN MATE FOR LIFE AND PERFORM ELABORATE COURTSHIP DANCES TO ATTRACT EACH OTHER.

SHARED DUTIES

ALBATROSSES LAY LARGE EGGS, AND BOTH PARENTS TAKE TURNS INCUBATING THE EGG UNTIL IT HATCHES. THE CHICK IS CARED FOR BY BOTH PARENTS UNTIL IT'S READY TO FLY.

RHINOCEROSES

BIG AND HEAVY

RHINOCEROSES, OR RHINOS FOR SHORT, ARE SOME OF THE LARGEST LAND ANIMALS. SOME SPECIES, LIKE THE WHITE RHINO, CAN WEIGH OVER 5,000 POUNDS, WHICH IS AS HEAVY AS A SMALL CAR!

HORNED HEROES

RHINOS HAVE ONE OR TWO HORNS ON THEIR NOSES, DEPENDING ON THE SPECIES. THESE HORNS ARE MADE OF KERATIN, THE SAME STUFF AS YOUR HAIR AND NAILS!

Rollin' in the Mud

RHINOS LOVE ROLLING IN MUD! IT KEEPS THEM COOL, PROTECTS THEIR SKIN FROM THE SUN, AND HELPS KEEP PESKY BUGS AWAY.

GENTLE GIANTS

RHINOS MIGHT LOOK TOUGH, BUT THEY'RE USUALLY CALM AND PEACEFUL ANIMALS UNLESS THEY FEEL THREATENED.

COYOTES

Brains and Brawn

COYOTES ARE PART OF THE DOG FAMILY, AND THEY'RE SUPER SMART AND ADAPTABLE. THEY CAN LIVE IN FORESTS, DESERTS, MOUNTAINS, AND EVEN CITIES!

VOICES OF THE WILD

COYOTES ARE KNOWN FOR THEIR HOWLS, YIPS, AND BARKS. THEY USE THESE SOUNDS TO COMMUNICATE WITH OTHER COYOTES AND MARK THEIR TERRITORY.

Built for Speed

COYOTES CAN RUN UP TO 40 MILES PER HOUR! THIS HELPS THEM CHASE PREY OR ESCAPE FROM DANGER.

MYTHICAL MISCHIEF

IN MANY NATIVE AMERICAN STORIES, COYOTES ARE KNOWN AS TRICKSTERS, OFTEN PLAYING CLEVER OR MISCHIEVOUS ROLES IN MYTHS AND LEGENDS.

ORCAS

BLENDING IN

THEIR BLACK-AND-WHITE COLORING HELPS THEM BLEND IN WITH THEIR SURROUNDINGS, MAKING IT HARDER FOR PREY TO SPOT THEM.

UNDERWATER CHATTER

ORCAS COMMUNICATE WITH CLICKS, WHISTLES, AND CALLS. EACH POD (FAMILY GROUP) HAS ITS OWN UNIQUE SET OF SOUNDS, LIKE A SECRET LANGUAGE!

The Dolphin Giants

ORCAS ARE OFTEN CALLED KILLER WHALES, BUT THEY'RE ACTUALLY THE LARGEST MEMBERS OF THE DOLPHIN FAMILY!

TOP PREDATORS

ORCAS ARE AT THE TOP OF THE FOOD CHAIN IN THE OCEAN. THEY HAVE NO NATURAL PREDATORS AND ARE SOMETIMES CALLED "APEX PREDATORS."

ANTELOPES

From Tiny to Giant

THERE ARE OVER 90 SPECIES OF ANTELOPES, RANGING FROM TINY ONES LIKE THE DIK-DIK TO LARGE ONES LIKE THE ELAND!

SPEEDY RUNNERS

ANTELOPES ARE BUILT FOR SPEED. SOME, LIKE THE PRONGHORN ANTELOPE, CAN RUN UP TO 55 MILES PER HOUR TO ESCAPE PREDATORS!

SHARP AND STYLISH

MOST ANTELOPES HAVE BEAUTIFUL CURVED OR SPIRAL-SHAPED HORNS. UNLIKE DEER, THEIR HORNS DON'T FALL OFF AND GROW BACK EACH YEAR.

Leap of Faith

ANTELOPES ARE GREAT AT JUMPING. THEY CAN LEAP OVER BUSHES AND ROCKS TO GET AWAY FROM DANGER OR JUST FOR FUN!

GRASSHOPPERS

AMAZING JUMPERS

GRASSHOPPERS ARE INCREDIBLE JUMPERS! THEY CAN LEAP UP TO 20 TIMES THEIR OWN BODY LENGTH IN A SINGLE JUMP.

Chirp, Chirp

MALE GRASSHOPPERS MAKE CHIRPING SOUNDS BY RUBBING THEIR BACK LEGS AGAINST THEIR WINGS. THEY DO THIS TO ATTRACT FEMALE GRASSHOPPERS.

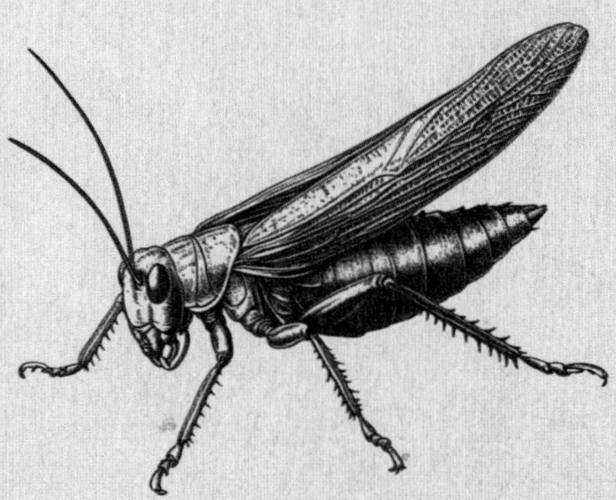

WINGING IT

GRASSHOPPERS HAVE TWO SETS OF WINGS: ONE FOR FLYING AND ONE FOR PROTECTION. THEY USE THEIR WINGS TO GLIDE THROUGH THE AIR WHEN THEY JUMP.

Ancient Survivors

GRASSHOPPERS HAVE BEEN AROUND FOR MILLIONS OF YEARS, EVEN BEFORE THE DINOSAURS! THEY'VE HARDLY CHANGED OVER TIME.

JELLYFISH

No Bones, No Brain

JELLYFISH DON'T HAVE BONES, A BRAIN, OR EVEN A HEART! THEY'RE MADE MOSTLY OF WATER AND JELLY-LIKE TISSUE.

FISHY NAME

EVEN THOUGH THEY'RE CALLED JELLYFISH, THEY'RE NOT ACTUALLY FISH. THEY BELONG TO A GROUP OF ANIMALS CALLED CNIDARIANS.

GLOW AND GO

SOME JELLYFISH CAN GLOW IN THE DARK THROUGH A PROCESS CALLED BIOLUMINESCENCE. THIS HELPS THEM ATTRACT PREY OR SCARE OFF PREDATORS.

Tentacles with Stingers

JELLYFISH HAVE LONG TENTACLES WITH TINY STINGERS TO CATCH THEIR FOOD. THEY USE THEIR STINGERS TO INJECT VENOM INTO SMALL FISH AND PLANKTON.

CATS

MILK MYTHS

CATS DON'T ACTUALLY NEED MILK, AND IT CAN UPSET THEIR STOMACHS. FRESH WATER IS MUCH BETTER FOR THEM.

CLEANING MACHINES

CATS SPEND ABOUT HALF THEIR DAY GROOMING THEMSELVES TO STAY CLEAN AND HEALTHY. THEIR ROUGH TONGUES HELP REMOVE DIRT AND LOOSE FUR.

Whisker Sensors

A CAT'S WHISKERS HELP THEM SENSE THEIR SURROUNDINGS. THEY CAN EVEN USE THEM TO MEASURE IF THEY'LL FIT THROUGH A SPACE!

NIGHT VISION

CATS CAN SEE IN THE DARK MUCH BETTER THAN HUMANS. THEIR EYES ARE SPECIALLY DESIGNED TO WORK WELL IN LOW LIGHT.

BUTTERFLIES

FLUTTERY FRIENDS

BUTTERFLIES ARE IMPORTANT POLLINATORS, HELPING PLANTS GROW BY SPREADING POLLEN AS THEY MOVE FROM FLOWER TO FLOWER.

Lots of Species

THERE ARE ABOUT 20,000 SPECIES OF BUTTERFLIES WORLDWIDE, LIVING IN FORESTS, MEADOWS, DESERTS, AND EVEN CITIES.

SUPER SIPPERS

BUTTERFLIES DRINK NECTAR FROM FLOWERS USING A LONG, STRAW-LIKE TONGUE CALLED A PROBOSCIS.

TASTY TOES

BUTTERFLIES HAVE TASTE BUDS ON THEIR FEET! THEY CAN LAND ON A PLANT AND INSTANTLY TELL IF IT'S GOOD TO EAT.

BODY ARMOR

BUTTERFLIES HAVE THEIR SKELETONS ON THE OUTSIDE OF THEIR BODIES! THIS HARD OUTER SHELL, CALLED AN EXOSKELETON, PROTECTS THEM AND KEEPS THEIR BODIES SAFE.

Tiny Travelers

MONARCH BUTTERFLIES MIGRATE THOUSANDS OF MILES EVERY YEAR, FLYING FROM THE UNITED STATES AND CANADA TO MEXICO.

FAKE EYES

SOME BUTTERFLIES HAVE SPOTS ON THEIR WINGS THAT LOOK LIKE BIG EYES TO SCARE OFF PREDATORS. IT'S LIKE HAVING BUILT-IN MASKS FOR SAFETY!

From Caterpillar to Butterfly

BUTTERFLIES GO THROUGH AN AMAZING TRANSFORMATION CALLED METAMORPHOSIS, STARTING AS EGGS, HATCHING INTO CATERPILLARS, FORMING A CHRYSALIS, AND FINALLY BECOMING BUTTERFLIES.

LEOPARDS

Anything on the Menu

LEOPARDS ARE NOT PICKY EATERS. THEY HUNT A WIDE RANGE OF ANIMALS, FROM SMALL BIRDS AND RODENTS TO LARGER ANIMALS LIKE DEER.

SPOTTED STYLE

LEOPARDS HAVE BEAUTIFUL GOLDEN COATS COVERED WITH BLACK SPOTS CALLED ROSETTES. THESE HELP THEM BLEND INTO THEIR SURROUNDINGS.

ME, MYSELF, AND I

LEOPARDS USUALLY LIVE AND HUNT ALONE, EXCEPT FOR MOTHERS RAISING THEIR CUBS. THEY LIKE TO KEEP THEIR SPACE AND MARK THEIR TERRITORY.

LAND OR WATER

WHILE THEY PREFER LAND, LEOPARDS ARE STRONG SWIMMERS AND WILL CROSS RIVERS OR STREAMS IF THEY NEED TO.

HEDGEHOGS

TINY FEET, BIG SPEED

EVEN THOUGH THEY HAVE TINY LEGS, HEDGEHOGS CAN RUN SURPRISINGLY FAST, ESPECIALLY WHEN THEY'RE SEARCHING FOR FOOD OR TRYING TO ESCAPE DANGER.

Spiky Superstars

HEDGEHOGS HAVE ABOUT 5,000 TO 7,000 SPINES ON THEIR BACKS! THESE SPINES HELP PROTECT THEM FROM PREDATORS.

SELF-ANOINTING MYSTERIES

HEDGEHOGS SOMETIMES LICK AND CHEW NEW THINGS THEY FIND, THEN SPREAD THE FROTHY SALIVA ON THEIR SPINES. SCIENTISTS AREN'T SURE WHY, BUT IT MIGHT HELP WITH PROTECTION OR SCENT MARKING.

HIBERNATE AND CHILL

IN COLDER CLIMATES, HEDGEHOGS HIBERNATE DURING THE WINTER. THEY SLEEP FOR MONTHS TO SAVE ENERGY WHEN FOOD IS HARD TO FIND.

ANTEATERS

SOLO TRAVELERS

ANTEATERS USUALLY LIVE ALONE, EXCEPT FOR MOMS WITH THEIR BABIES. THEY SPEND MOST OF THEIR TIME WANDERING IN SEARCH OF FOOD.

Baby Riders

WHEN BABY ANTEATERS ARE BORN, THEY RIDE ON THEIR MOM'S BACK FOR SEVERAL MONTHS, CLINGING TIGHTLY WITH THEIR TINY CLAWS.

TONGUE-TASTIC!

ANTEATERS HAVE SUPER LONG TONGUES UP TO TWO FEET! THEIR TONGUES ARE STICKY, WHICH HELPS THEM SCOOP UP THOUSANDS OF ANTS AND TERMITES IN MINUTES.

LONG SNOUTS

ANTEATERS HAVE LONG SNOUTS THAT HOUSE THEIR LONG TONGUES. THEIR SNOUTS HELP THEM REACH DEEP INTO ANT NESTS.

LLAMAS

Mountain Masters

LLAMAS ARE BUILT FOR LIFE IN THE MOUNTAINS. THEY'RE SURE-FOOTED AND CAN EASILY WALK ON ROCKY TRAILS.

LLAMA DRAMA

LLAMAS HUM TO COMMUNICATE WITH EACH OTHER. A HAPPY LLAMA MIGHT HUM SOFTLY, WHILE A GRUMPY ONE MIGHT MAKE LOUDER, FUNNY NOISES.

SPIT HAPPENS

LLAMAS SPIT WHEN THEY FEEL ANNOYED OR NEED TO SHOW WHO'S BOSS. DON'T WORRY—THEY MOSTLY SPIT AT OTHER LLAMAS, NOT PEOPLE!

Meet the Llama Family

LLAMAS ARE PART OF THE CAMEL FAMILY AND ARE COUSINS TO ALPACAS, GUANACOS, AND VICUNAS.

HORSES

UNIQUE HOOVES

A HORSE'S HOOF IS MADE OF KERATIN, THE SAME MATERIAL AS HUMAN FINGERNAILS. HOOVES NEED TO BE TRIMMED REGULARLY TO STAY HEALTHY.

Big Hearts

A HORSE'S HEART IS HUGE—IT CAN WEIGH UP TO TEN POUNDS, HELPING THEM PUMP BLOOD QUICKLY WHILE THEY RUN.

WHINNY AND NEIGH

HORSES MAKE DIFFERENT SOUNDS, LIKE WHINNIES, NEIGHS, AND SNORTS, TO EXPRESS HOW THEY FEEL AND COMMUNICATE WITH EACH OTHER.

SUPER SENSES

HORSES HAVE EXCELLENT HEARING AND EYESIGHT. THEIR WIDE-SET EYES LET THEM SEE ALMOST ALL THE WAY AROUND THEMSELVES!

PIGS

Farmyard Geniuses

PIGS HAVE GREAT MEMORIES. THEY CAN REMEMBER AND RECOGNIZE THEIR HUMAN CARETAKERS AND EVEN NAVIGATE THROUGH MAZES OR REMEMBER PLACES WHERE FOOD IS HIDDEN!

NOT DIRTY JUST COOL

CONTRARY TO POPULAR BELIEF, PIGS ARE ACTUALLY QUITE CLEAN. THEY KEEP THEIR SLEEPING AREAS TIDY AND ONLY ROLL IN THE MUD TO STAY COOL OR PROTECT THEMSELVES FROM SUNBURNS AND BUGS.

Incredible Snouts

PIGS HAVE A FANTASTIC SENSE OF SMELL, THANKS TO THEIR STRONG SNOUTS. THEIR NOSES ARE SO SENSITIVE THEY CAN SNIFF OUT TRUFFLES (A TYPE OF FUNGUS) UNDERGROUND!

PADDLING PIGS

PIGS ARE SURPRISINGLY GOOD SWIMMERS! THEY CAN PADDLE THROUGH WATER TO COOL OFF AND EVEN ENJOY SWIMMING IN PONDS OR LAKES.

OSTRICHES

From Tall to Mighty

OSTRICHES ARE THE LARGEST BIRDS IN THE WORLD! THEY CAN GROW UP TO 9 FEET TALL AND WEIGH UP TO 350 POUNDS.

SPEED STARS

OSTRICHES ARE INCREDIBLE RUNNERS. THEY CAN RUN AT SPEEDS OF UP TO 45 MILES PER HOUR, WHICH MAKES THEM THE FASTEST RUNNING BIRD ON LAND!

FLUFFY AND FUNCTIONAL

OSTRICHES HAVE SOFT, FLUFFY FEATHERS THAT HELP KEEP THEM COOL IN HOT CLIMATES. THEIR FEATHERS ARE DIFFERENT FROM MOST OTHER BIRDS BECAUSE THEY DON'T HAVE THE USUAL STIFF STRUCTURE.

Flightless Wonders

UNLIKE MANY OTHER BIRDS, OSTRICHES CANNOT FLY. BUT THEY ARE GREAT AT RUNNING AND CAN COVER A LOT OF GROUND QUICKLY.

SHEEP

WOOLLY COATS

SHEEP ARE KNOWN FOR THEIR THICK, WOOLLY COATS. THEIR WOOL KEEPS THEM WARM IN THE WINTER AND COOL IN THE SUMMER. IT'S OFTEN USED TO MAKE CLOTHING LIKE SWEATERS AND SOCKS!

SAFETY IN NUMBERS

SHEEP ARE VERY SOCIAL ANIMALS AND PREFER TO LIVE IN HERDS. THEY STICK TOGETHER FOR SAFETY AND TO FIND FOOD, AND THEY FOLLOW EACH OTHER CLOSELY.

MEET THE FLOCK

FEMALE SHEEP ARE CALLED EWES, AND BABY SHEEP ARE CALLED LAMBS. A GROUP OF SHEEP IS CALLED A FLOCK.

Fleece Facts

NOT ALL SHEEP HAVE THE SAME TYPE OF WOOL. SOME PRODUCE SOFT WOOL USED FOR MAKING FINE CLOTHING, WHILE OTHERS HAVE COARSER WOOL USED FOR MAKING BLANKETS AND CARPETS.

MONKEYS

SUPER SWINGERS

MANY MONKEYS, LIKE SPIDER MONKEYS, USE THEIR STRONG, PREHENSILE TAILS LIKE AN EXTRA ARM TO SWING AND GRIP BRANCHES IN THE TREES.

Jungle Dwellers

MOST MONKEYS LIVE IN TROPICAL RAINFORESTS, BUT SOME, LIKE SNOW MONKEYS, LIVE IN COLD, SNOWY MOUNTAINS.

COUSINS, NOT TWINS

MONKEYS AND APES ARE NOT THE SAME, BUT THEY ARE PART OF THE SAME PRIMATE FAMILY TREE AND SHARE MANY SIMILARITIES.

TREE OR GROUND

SOME MONKEYS, LIKE HOWLER MONKEYS, RARELY LEAVE THE TREES, WHILE OTHERS, LIKE BABOONS, SPEND MOST OF THEIR TIME ON THE GROUND.

CHEEK POUCHES

MONKEYS LIKE MACAQUES HAVE CHEEK POUCHES TO STORE FOOD FOR SNACKING LATER.

Planet of the Monkeys

THERE ARE OVER 260 DIFFERENT TYPES OF MONKEYS LIVING ALL AROUND THE WORLD, EACH WITH UNIQUE FEATURES AND BEHAVIORS SUITED TO THEIR ENVIRONMENTS.

SMART COOKIES

MONKEYS ARE REALLY SMART! THEY CAN USE TOOLS, SOLVE PUZZLES, AND EVEN LEARN TO COMMUNICATE WITH HUMANS.

Monkey See, Monkey Do

MONKEYS ARE GREAT AT COPYING! THEY OFTEN IMITATE EACH OTHER AND SOMETIMES EVEN HUMANS, LEARNING NEW SKILLS BY WATCHING AND MIMICKING WHAT OTHERS DO.

WOMBATS

Digging Machines

WOMBATS ARE EXCELLENT DIGGERS. THEY USE THEIR STRONG CLAWS TO DIG BURROWS WHERE THEY SLEEP AND STAY SAFE FROM PREDATORS. SOME BURROWS CAN BE UP TO 100 FEET LONG!

CHUNKY CHARMERS

WOMBATS ARE SMALL, STOCKY MARSUPIALS THAT LOOK A BIT LIKE TINY BEARS. THEY HAVE SHORT, THICK LEGS AND A CUTE, ROUNDED BODY THAT HELPS THEM DIG TUNNELS.

CUBE CRAZE

ONE OF THE MOST UNUSUAL FACTS ABOUT WOMBATS IS THAT THEIR POOP IS CUBE-SHAPED! THIS HELPS IT STAY IN PLACE AND MARK THEIR TERRITORY. THE SHAPE IS CAUSED BY THEIR SLOW DIGESTIVE SYSTEM.

Slow Metabolism, Big Advantage

WOMBATS HAVE A SLOW METABOLISM, MEANING IT TAKES A LONG TIME FOR THEM TO DIGEST FOOD. IT CAN TAKE UP TO TWO WEEKS FOR FOOD TO FULLY PASS THROUGH THEIR BODIES!

WEASELS

Small Size, Big Moves

WEASELS ARE SMALL, SLENDER ANIMALS THAT ARE KNOWN FOR THEIR AGILITY AND QUICK MOVEMENTS. THEY CAN SQUEEZE INTO TINY SPACES AND ARE VERY GOOD AT SNEAKING AROUND!

BUILT TO HUNT

WEASELS HAVE SHARP TEETH AND CLAWS THAT HELP THEM CATCH AND HOLD ONTO THEIR PREY. THEY USE THEIR SHARP TEETH TO KILL AND EAT THEIR FOOD.

Global Travelers

WEASELS ARE FOUND IN MANY PARTS OF THE WORLD, INCLUDING FORESTS, GRASSLANDS, AND EVEN URBAN AREAS. THEY LIVE IN NORTH AMERICA, EUROPE, ASIA, AND PARTS OF AFRICA.

TINY BODIES, BIG APPETITES

WEASELS HAVE VERY FAST METABOLISMS, MEANING THEY NEED TO EAT A LOT OF FOOD TO KEEP THEIR ENERGY UP. THEY OFTEN HUNT THROUGHOUT THE DAY AND NIGHT TO GET ENOUGH FOOD.

SEALS

FLIPPER POWER

SEALS' FRONT AND BACK FLIPPERS HELP THEM SWIM GRACEFULLY IN THE WATER, BUT ON LAND, THEY WIGGLE AND FLOP AROUND TO MOVE.

Deep Divers

SEALS ARE AMAZING SWIMMERS! THEY CAN DIVE DEEP UNDERWATER AND SWIM FAST USING THEIR STRONG FLIPPERS.

Playful and Curious

SEALS ARE KNOWN FOR BEING PLAYFUL AND CURIOUS. THEY LOVE TO EXPLORE AND SOMETIMES EVEN INTERACT WITH DIVERS AND BOATS!

NO AIR NEEDED

SOME SEALS, LIKE ELEPHANT SEALS, CAN DIVE OVER 5,000 FEET DEEP IN THE OCEAN AND STAY UNDERWATER FOR UP TO TWO HOURS!

CARIBOU

ONE SPECIES, MANY NAMES

CARIBOU AND REINDEER ARE THE SAME SPECIES! IN NORTH AMERICA, THEY'RE CALLED CARIBOU, WHILE IN EUROPE AND ASIA, THEY'RE KNOWN AS REINDEER.

BIG HERDS

CARIBOU LIVE IN LARGE HERDS, SOMETIMES WITH THOUSANDS OF ANIMALS TRAVELING TOGETHER. THIS HELPS PROTECT THEM FROM PREDATORS.

Built for Snow

CARIBOU HAVE WIDE, ROUNDED HOOVES THAT ACT LIKE SNOWSHOES, HELPING THEM WALK ON SNOW AND SOFT GROUND WITHOUT SINKING.

ANTLER EQUALITY

UNLIKE MOST DEER, BOTH MALE AND FEMALE CARIBOU GROW ANTLERS. MALES USE THEIRS TO BATTLE FOR MATES, WHILE FEMALES USE THEIRS TO PROTECT FOOD DURING WINTER.

CHIPMUNKS

Snacks to Go

CHIPMUNKS HAVE STRETCHY CHEEK POUCHES WHERE THEY CAN STORE FOOD LIKE NUTS AND SEEDS. THEY CARRY THEIR SNACKS BACK TO THEIR BURROWS TO SAVE FOR LATER.

TINY TROTTERS

CHIPMUNKS ARE SMALL RODENTS, USUALLY ABOUT THE SIZE OF YOUR HAND, BUT THEY'RE SUPER ACTIVE AND FULL OF ENERGY!

STYLISH STRIPES

CHIPMUNKS HAVE DISTINCTIVE STRIPES RUNNING DOWN THEIR BACKS. THESE STRIPES HELP THEM BLEND IN WITH THEIR SURROUNDINGS TO STAY HIDDEN FROM PREDATORS.

Power Naps

UNLIKE SOME ANIMALS, CHIPMUNKS DON'T FULLY HIBERNATE. INSTEAD, THEY TAKE SHORT NAPS IN THEIR BURROWS AND WAKE UP TO SNACK ON THEIR STORED FOOD.

LIZARDS

LIZARDS GALORE

THERE ARE MORE THAN 6,000 DIFFERENT TYPES OF LIZARDS, FROM TINY GECKOS TO GIANT KOMODO DRAGONS!

STICKY TOES

SOME LIZARDS, LIKE GECKOS, HAVE SPECIAL TOE PADS THAT LET THEM CLIMB WALLS AND EVEN HANG UPSIDE DOWN.

No Blinking Needed

SOME LIZARDS, DON'T HAVE EYELIDS. INSTEAD, THEY USE THEIR TONGUES TO LICK THEIR EYES AND KEEP THEM CLEAN AND MOIST!

SCALY SURVIVORS

LIZARDS ARE DISTANT RELATIVES OF DINOSAURS. THEIR SCALY SKIN AND ANCIENT LINEAGE MAKE THEM LOOK LIKE MINIATURE VERSIONS OF THOSE PREHISTORIC GIANTS.

DRAGONFLIES

Bug-Eye View

DRAGONFLIES HAVE HUGE EYES THAT COVER MOST OF THEIR HEAD. THEY CAN SEE ALMOST ALL THE WAY AROUND THEM, HELPING THEM SPOT PREY AND AVOID PREDATORS.

FROM WATER TO SKY

DRAGONFLIES SPEND MOST OF THEIR LIVES UNDERWATER AS NYMPHS (BABY DRAGONFLIES), WHERE THEY HUNT SMALL WATER CREATURES. THEY ONLY LIVE A FEW MONTHS AS ADULTS.

Two Sets of Wings

DRAGONFLIES HAVE TWO SETS OF WINGS THAT WORK INDEPENDENTLY, GIVING THEM INCREDIBLE CONTROL AND SPEED IN THE AIR.

NO BITE, NO STING

EVEN THOUGH THEY LOOK FIERCE, DRAGONFLIES DON'T STING OR BITE HUMANS. THEY'RE COMPLETELY HARMLESS TO PEOPLE.

EAGLES

Amazing Eyesight

EAGLES HAVE INCREDIBLE VISION! THEY CAN SEE FOUR TO EIGHT TIMES FARTHER THAN HUMANS AND SPOT A RABBIT FROM OVER A MILE AWAY.

SYMBOL OF STRENGTH

IN MANY CULTURES, EAGLES ARE SYMBOLS OF POWER AND FREEDOM. THE BALD EAGLE IS THE NATIONAL BIRD OF THE UNITED STATES.

Masters of the Sky

EAGLES CAN SOAR FOR HOURS WITHOUT FLAPPING THEIR WINGS, USING AIR CURRENTS TO GLIDE HIGH ABOVE THE GROUND.

GREAT FISHERMEN

MANY EAGLES, LIKE THE BALD EAGLE, ARE EXCELLENT AT CATCHING FISH. THEY SWOOP DOWN, SNATCH THE FISH WITH THEIR TALONS, AND FLY OFF TO EAT IT.

WHALES

DEEP DIVERS

SPERM WHALES CAN DIVE MORE THAN 7,000 FEET DEEP IN SEARCH OF THEIR FAVORITE FOOD, GIANT SQUID.

SINGERS, SONGWRITERS

HUMPBACK WHALES SING LONG, COMPLEX SONGS TO COMMUNICATE. SOME SONGS CAN LAST FOR HOURS!

The Biggest Creature in the Ocean

BLUE WHALES ARE THE LARGEST ANIMALS ON EARTH, GROWING UP TO 100 FEET LONG AND WEIGHING AS MUCH AS 30 ELEPHANTS!

BLOWHOLE BREATHERS

WHALES BREATHE AIR THROUGH A BLOWHOLE ON TOP OF THEIR HEADS, MAKING IT EASY TO COME UP FOR A QUICK BREATH.

POD LIFE

WHALES ARE SOCIAL AND LIVE IN GROUPS CALLED PODS, WHERE THEY COMMUNICATE AND WORK TOGETHER.

Echo Experts

TOOTHED WHALES, LIKE DOLPHINS AND ORCAS, USE ECHOLOCATION TO "SEE" UNDERWATER BY BOUNCING SOUND WAVES OFF OBJECTS.

TOOTH OR BALEEN

SOME WHALES, LIKE SPERM WHALES, HAVE TEETH, WHILE OTHERS, LIKE BLUE WHALES, HAVE BALEEN PLATES TO FILTER TINY FOOD FROM THE WATER.

Warm-Blooded Giants

WHALES ARE MAMMALS, JUST LIKE US! THEY'RE WARM-BLOODED, GIVE BIRTH TO LIVE BABIES, AND NURSE THEIR YOUNG WITH MILK.

GIRAFFES

LONG NECKS, FEW BONES

EVEN THOUGH THEIR NECKS ARE SUPER LONG, GIRAFFES HAVE ONLY SEVEN NECK BONES, JUST LIKE HUMANS. THEIR BONES ARE MUCH BIGGER, THOUGH!

Tallest Animals on Land

GIRAFFES ARE THE TALLEST ANIMALS ON EARTH! THEY CAN GROW UP TO 18 FEET TALL, WITH THEIR LONG NECKS MAKING UP A BIG PART OF THEIR HEIGHT.

SUPER TONGUES

GIRAFFES HAVE LONG, DARK-COLORED TONGUES THAT CAN BE UP TO 20 INCHES LONG. THEY USE THEIR TONGUES TO GRAB LEAVES FROM TALL TREES.

GROUP LIVING

GIRAFFES LIVE IN GROUPS CALLED TOWERS. THESE GROUPS ARE USUALLY MADE UP OF FEMALES AND THEIR CALVES, WITH MALES COMING AND GOING.

PANDAS

BAMBOO LOVERS

PANDAS EAT MOSTLY BAMBOO! THEY CAN MUNCH ON UP TO 40 POUNDS OF IT EVERY DAY, EVEN THOUGH THEY ARE TECHNICALLY CARNIVORES.

China's Treasure

PANDAS ARE A NATIONAL SYMBOL OF CHINA AND ARE OFTEN CALLED "AMBASSADORS OF PEACE" BECAUSE THEY'RE SO LOVED AROUND THE WORLD.

THUMBS UP!

PANDAS HAVE A SPECIAL "THUMB" (WHICH IS ACTUALLY AN EXTENDED WRIST BONE) TO HELP THEM HOLD AND STRIP BAMBOO STALKS.

Black, White, and Blending In

PANDAS ARE FAMOUS FOR THEIR BLACK AND WHITE FUR. THEIR UNIQUE PATTERN HELPS THEM BLEND INTO THEIR SNOWY AND ROCKY FOREST HABITATS.

CHINCHILLAS

NATURAL JUMPERS

CHINCHILLAS ARE AMAZING JUMPERS. THEY CAN LEAP UP TO SIX FEET HIGH TO ESCAPE PREDATORS OR EXPLORE THEIR SURROUNDINGS.

Big Whiskers

THEIR LONG WHISKERS HELP THEM FEEL AROUND IN THE DARK AND NAVIGATE TIGHT SPACES WITHOUT BUMPING INTO THINGS.

Rolling in Dust

INSTEAD OF TAKING WATER BATHS, CHINCHILLAS ROLL AROUND IN SPECIAL DUST TO KEEP THEIR FUR CLEAN AND HEALTHY.

BORN IN THE ANDES

CHINCHILLAS COME FROM THE ANDES MOUNTAINS IN SOUTH AMERICA, WHERE THEY LIVE IN ROCKY, COLD ENVIRONMENTS.

PLATYPUS

NO STOMACH

UNLIKE MOST ANIMALS, PLATYPUSES DON'T HAVE A STOMACH, SO THEIR FOOD GOES STRAIGHT FROM THEIR ESOPHAGUS TO THEIR INTESTINES, WHERE IT IS DIGESTED WITHOUT THE NEED FOR ACID BREAKDOWN.

GRAVEL GOURMETS

PLATYPUSES DON'T HAVE TEETH! INSTEAD, THEY SCOOP UP GRAVEL AND USE IT TO GRIND THEIR FOOD WHILE SWIMMING.

Clumsy but Cute

PLATYPUSES WADDLE AWKWARDLY ON LAND BECAUSE THEIR WEBBED FEET FOLD UP, TURNING INTO CLAWS FOR WALKING, WHICH HELPS THEM GRIP THE GROUND BUT MAKES THEIR MOVEMENT LOOK CLUMSY.

VENOMOUS SPURS

MALE PLATYPUSES HAVE VENOMOUS SPURS ON THEIR BACK LEGS. WHILE THE VENOM ISN'T DEADLY TO HUMANS, IT CAN CAUSE A LOT OF PAIN!

MEERKATS

Standing Watch

MEERKATS ARE FAMOUS FOR STANDING UPRIGHT ON THEIR HIND LEGS. THEY DO THIS TO KEEP A LOOKOUT FOR PREDATORS LIKE HAWKS AND SNAKES.

TEAM PLAYERS

WHILE SOME MEERKATS WATCH FOR DANGER, OTHERS DIG FOR FOOD OR TAKE CARE OF THE BABIES. THEY WORK TOGETHER TO KEEP THEIR FAMILY SAFE AND FED.

Immune to Venom

MEERKATS HAVE A SPECIAL RESISTANCE TO SCORPION VENOM, SO THEY CAN SAFELY EAT SCORPIONS WITHOUT GETTING HURT.

THE MOB LIFE

MEERKATS ARE TINY MAMMALS, ABOUT THE SIZE OF A SQUIRREL, AND THEY LOVE LIVING IN BIG FAMILIES CALLED MOBS OR CLANS, WHICH CAN HAVE UP TO 30 MEMBERS!

SQUIDS

Ink Escape Artists

WHEN THREATENED, GIANT SQUIDS CAN RELEASE A CLOUD OF DARK INK TO CONFUSE PREDATORS LIKE SPERM WHALES, THEIR MAIN ENEMIES.

TENTACLE TITANS

WITH EIGHT ARMS AND TWO SUPER-LONG TENTACLES, GIANT SQUIDS USE THEIR SUCTION CUPS TO GRAB PREY UP TO 30 FEET AWAY.

JET PROPULSION

THEY MOVE THROUGH THE WATER BY SHOOTING OUT A JET OF WATER FROM THEIR BODIES, HELPING THEM ESCAPE QUICKLY IF NEEDED.

Biggest Eyes in the Animal Kingdom

GIANT SQUIDS HAVE THE LARGEST EYES OF ANY ANIMAL, ABOUT THE SIZE OF A BASKETBALL! THESE BIG EYES HELP THEM SEE IN THE DARK, DEEP OCEAN.

RABBITS

Fast Hoppers

RABBITS CAN HOP UP TO 35 MILES PER HOUR, MAKING THEM INCREDIBLY SPEEDY AND AGILE WHEN ESCAPING DANGER OR DASHING TO SAFETY IN THEIR BURROWS.

TWITCHY NOSES

A RABBIT'S NOSE TWITCHES ALL THE TIME TO HELP THEM SMELL BETTER, DETECT SCENTS IN THE AIR, AND STAY ALERT FOR DANGER.

Underground Homes

WILD RABBITS LIVE IN BURROWS OR WARRENS, WHICH ARE TUNNELS THEY DIG UNDERGROUND TO STAY SAFE AND COZY.

BIG FAMILIES

RABBITS CAN HAVE LOTS OF BABIES, CALLED KITS, AND THEY GROW UP FAST! A MOTHER RABBIT, OR DOE, CAN GIVE BIRTH TO UP TO 12 KITS AT A TIME, MAKING RABBITS KNOWN FOR THEIR BIG FAMILIES.

DOGS

SUPER SMELLERS

DOGS HAVE AN AMAZING SENSE OF SMELL—UP TO 100,000 TIMES BETTER THAN HUMANS! THEY USE THEIR NOSES TO SNIFF OUT FOOD, PEOPLE, AND EVEN EMOTIONS.

DOGS DREAM

JUST LIKE HUMANS, DOGS DREAM WHEN THEY SLEEP! YOU MIGHT SEE THEIR LEGS TWITCHING AS THEY CHASE IMAGINARY SQUIRRELS IN THEIR DREAMS.

SMARTY PAWS

DOGS CAN LEARN OVER 100 WORDS OR COMMANDS, AND SOME SUPER-SMART DOGS EVEN KNOW MORE THAN 200!

Oldest Dog Breeds

SOME DOG BREEDS, LIKE THE SALUKI, HAVE BEEN AROUND FOR THOUSANDS OF YEARS, MAKING THEM SOME OF THE OLDEST KNOWN BREEDS.

SHARKS

TOOTHY GRINS

A SHARK CAN GROW AND LOSE THOUSANDS OF TEETH IN ITS LIFETIME. SOME EVEN HAVE ROWS OF BACKUP TEETH READY TO GO!

Big, Small, and Everything in Between

THERE ARE OVER 500 SPECIES OF SHARKS IN THE WORLD, FROM TINY LANTERN SHARKS TO MASSIVE WHALE SHARKS!

ANCIENT PREDATORS

SHARKS HAVE BEEN AROUND FOR MORE THAN 400 MILLION YEARS, EVEN BEFORE DINOSAURS.

GIRL POWER

FEMALE GREAT WHITE SHARKS ARE BIGGER THAN MALES! THEY CAN GROW UP TO 20 FEET LONG, MAKING THEM THE QUEENS OF THE OCEAN.

NIGHT VISION

SOME SHARKS HAVE SPECIAL EYES THAT LET THEM SEE IN THE DARK! A SHINY LAYER IN THEIR EYES HELPS THEM HUNT IN DEEP, DARK WATERS WHERE IT'S HARD TO SEE.

Shark Pups

BABY SHARKS ARE CALLED PUPS, AND SOME SPECIES ARE BORN LIVE, WHILE OTHERS HATCH FROM EGGS.

NO BONES ABOUT IT

SHARKS DON'T HAVE BONES. THEIR SKELETONS ARE MADE OF CARTILAGE, THE SAME FLEXIBLE MATERIAL AS YOUR NOSE AND EARS.

Silent Swimmers

SHARKS DON'T HAVE VOCAL CORDS, SO THEY CAN'T MAKE ANY SOUNDS. INSTEAD, THEY RELY ON BODY LANGUAGE TO COMMUNICATE AND STAY STEALTHY WHILE HUNTING!

FLAMINGOS

Saltwater Survivors

FLAMINGOS CAN LIVE IN SALTY LAKES WHERE OTHER ANIMALS CAN'T. THEY HAVE SPECIAL GLANDS THAT HELP THEM GET RID OF EXTRA SALT FROM THEIR BODIES.

BUILT-IN FOOD FILTERS

FLAMINGOS HAVE SPECIAL BEAKS WITH BUILT-IN FILTERS. THEY USE THEM TO SCOOP UP WATER AND MUD, THEN FILTER OUT THE TASTY BITS LIKE SMALL SHRIMP AND PLANKTON.

DANCING DIVAS

TO ATTRACT MATES, FLAMINGOS PERFORM GROUP DANCES, MOVING IN SYNC AND SHOWING OFF THEIR BEAUTIFUL PLUMAGE.

PRETTY IN PINK

FLAMINGOS ARE FAMOUS FOR THEIR BRIGHT PINK FEATHERS. THEIR COLOR COMES FROM THE FOOD THEY EAT, LIKE SHRIMP AND ALGAE, WHICH ARE RICH IN A PIGMENT CALLED BETA-CAROTENE.

TURTLES

TURTLE SQUAD

THERE ARE OVER 300 SPECIES OF TURTLES, INCLUDING SEA TURTLES, LAND TURTLES, AND FRESHWATER TURTLES.

Not All Turtles Swim

WHILE MANY TURTLES LIVE IN WATER, SOME, LIKE BOX TURTLES, SPEND MOST OF THEIR TIME ON LAND.

MEMORY MASTERS

TURTLES ARE SMART! THEY CAN LEARN TO NAVIGATE MAZES AND REMEMBER THE PATHS FOR A LONG TIME.

Baby Turtles Find Their Way

WHEN BABY SEA TURTLES HATCH, THEY USE THE LIGHT OF THE MOON AND STARS TO GUIDE THEM TOWARD THE OCEAN. THIS NATURAL GLOW HELPS THEM NAVIGATE ACROSS THE SANDY BEACH AND INTO THE SAFETY OF THE WAVES.

FOXES

Solo Explorers

UNLIKE WOLVES, FOXES USUALLY HUNT AND LIVE ALONE, ALTHOUGH THEY MAY STAY WITH THEIR FAMILY FOR A SHORT TIME WHEN RAISING KITS (BABY FOXES).

NOCTURNAL EXPLORERS

FOXES ARE MOST ACTIVE AT NIGHT, RELYING ON THEIR SHARP SENSES TO HUNT AND EXPLORE IN THE DARK.

Foxy Fashion

NOT ALL FOXES ARE RED! SOME ARE WHITE, LIKE ARCTIC FOXES, WHILE OTHERS CAN BE GRAY OR EVEN BLACK WITH SILVER HIGHLIGHTS.

LEAPING LEGENDS

FOXES CAN JUMP HIGH AND FAR. THEY USE THEIR STRONG LEGS TO POUNCE ON PREY OR LEAP OVER OBSTACLES.

OTTERS

Family Bonds

RIVER OTTERS LIVE IN SMALL FAMILY GROUPS, WHILE SEA OTTERS OFTEN GATHER IN LARGER GROUPS CALLED RAFTS, WHICH CAN HAVE UP TO 100 OTTERS!

EXPERT FISHERMEN

OTTERS ARE AMAZING HUNTERS. THEY CATCH FISH, CRABS, AND OTHER WATER CREATURES WITH THEIR SHARP CLAWS AND QUICK REFLEXES.

Built-In Life Jackets

OTTERS HAVE THICK, WATERPROOF FUR THAT KEEPS THEM WARM AND HELPS THEM FLOAT IN COLD WATER.

WHISKER DETECTIVES

OTTERS HAVE SENSITIVE WHISKERS THAT HELP THEM DETECT MOVEMENTS IN THE WATER, MAKING IT EASIER TO FIND FOOD EVEN IN MURKY CONDITIONS.

DOLPHINS

Ocean Einsteins

DOLPHINS ARE ONE OF THE SMARTEST ANIMALS IN THE WORLD! THEY CAN SOLVE PUZZLES, LEARN TRICKS, AND EVEN RECOGNIZE THEMSELVES IN MIRRORS.

JUMP FOR JOY

JUMPING IS PART OF A DOLPHIN'S PLAYFUL BEHAVIOR, AND SCIENTISTS BELIEVE IT MIGHT EVEN HELP THEM BOND WITH THEIR POD.

Meet the Family

THERE ARE OVER 40 SPECIES OF DOLPHINS, INCLUDING THE BOTTLENOSE DOLPHIN, SPINNER DOLPHIN, AND EVEN RIVER DOLPHINS THAT LIVE IN FRESHWATER.

WAVE RIDERS

DOLPHINS OFTEN RIDE THE WAVES CREATED BY BOATS OR BIG WAVES IN THE OCEAN. IT'S LIKE THEIR VERSION OF SURFING!

BEAVERS

NATURE'S ARCHITECTS

BEAVERS ARE FAMOUS FOR BUILDING DAMS OUT OF WOOD, MUD, AND ROCKS. THESE DAMS CREATE PONDS WHERE THEY BUILD THEIR HOMES, CALLED LODGES.

WETLAND CREATORS

BEAVER DAMS CREATE WETLANDS THAT PROVIDE HOMES FOR MANY OTHER ANIMALS AND HELP KEEP WATER CLEAN AND PREVENT FLOODS.

Tails That Do It All

BEAVERS HAVE WIDE, FLAT TAILS THAT HELP THEM SWIM, BALANCE WHILE CUTTING TREES, AND EVEN WARN OTHER BEAVERS OF DANGER BY SLAPPING THE WATER.

COZY WATER HOMES

A BEAVER'S LODGE HAS UNDERWATER ENTRANCES TO KEEP PREDATORS OUT AND A COZY, DRY SPACE ABOVE THE WATER FOR THE FAMILY TO LIVE IN.

SKUNKS

SCENT-SATIONAL SHIELDS

SKUNKS ARE FAMOUS FOR THEIR STINKY SPRAY, WHICH THEY USE TO SCARE OFF PREDATORS. THEIR SPRAY CAN BE SMELLED UP TO A MILE AWAY!

SILENT WALKERS

SKUNKS ARE QUIET ANIMALS THAT SNEAK AROUND WHILE HUNTING FOR FOOD. THEIR SLOW, WADDLING WALK KEEPS THEM FROM DRAWING ATTENTION.

Nature's Warning Label

A SKUNK'S BLACK-AND-WHITE STRIPES ARE A WARNING SIGN TO PREDATORS THAT SAYS, "STAY BACK, OR ELSE!"

WARN FIRST, STINK LATER

SKUNKS ONLY SPRAY WHEN THEY FEEL THREATENED. THEY PREFER TO WARN PREDATORS FIRST BY STOMPING THEIR FEET OR RAISING THEIR TAILS.

AARDVARKS

Always First in Line

AARDVARKS ARE THE FIRST ANIMAL LISTED IN THE DICTIONARY BECAUSE THEIR NAME STARTS WITH TWO "A"S!

Fast and Fur-ious Diggers

WITH THEIR STRONG CLAWS, AARDVARKS CAN DIG SUPER FAST. THEY CAN DIG THROUGH DIRT AND MAKE A BURROW IN JUST MINUTES.

TERMITE TERMINATORS

AARDVARKS LOVE EATING ANTS AND TERMITES. IN FACT, THEY CAN EAT UP TO 50,000 ANTS IN ONE NIGHT!

NOSES THAT KNOW

AARDVARKS HAVE A GREAT SENSE OF SMELL TO HELP THEM SNIFF OUT BUGS, EVEN WHEN THEY'RE HIDING UNDERGROUND.

SNAKES

SO MANY SNAKES

THERE ARE OVER 3,900 SPECIES OF SNAKES IN THE WORLD, FOUND ON EVERY CONTINENT EXCEPT ANTARCTICA. THEY COME IN ALL SHAPES, SIZES, AND COLORS, FROM TINY THREADSNAKES TO MASSIVE ANACONDAS!

LARGEST SNAKE

THE GREEN ANACONDA IS THE HEAVIEST SNAKE, WHILE THE RETICULATED PYTHON IS THE LONGEST, GROWING OVER 30 FEET!

Scales for Survival

A SNAKE'S SCALES HELP PROTECT ITS BODY AND PROVIDE GRIP FOR CLIMBING OR MOVING ON SLIPPERY SURFACES.

NO LEGS, NO PROBLEM

SNAKES MOVE WITHOUT LEGS BY USING THEIR MUSCLES AND SCALES TO SLITHER, CLIMB, AND EVEN SWIM.

VENOM POWER

SOME SNAKES, LIKE COBRAS AND RATTLESNAKES, PRODUCE VENOM TO CATCH PREY OR DEFEND THEMSELVES.

Built-in Sunglasses

SNAKES HAVE A SPECIAL SCALE OVER THEIR EYES CALLED A SPECTACLE, WHICH PROTECTS THEIR EYES SINCE THEY DON'T HAVE EYELIDS.

SNAKE CHARM

COBRAS CAN "DANCE" TO THE MOVEMENTS OF A SNAKE CHARMER'S FLUTE, BUT THEY DON'T ACTUALLY HEAR THE MUSIC. THEY FOLLOW THE MOVEMENT INSTEAD.

Non-Venomous Strength

NON-VENOMOUS SNAKES, LIKE BOAS AND PYTHONS, USE THEIR POWERFUL MUSCLES TO SQUEEZE AND SUBDUE THEIR PREY.

ELEPHANTS

EARTH'S HEAVYWEIGHT CHAMPIONS

ELEPHANTS ARE THE LARGEST LAND ANIMALS ON EARTH! A FULLY GROWN AFRICAN ELEPHANT CAN WEIGH AS MUCH AS A SCHOOL BUS.

Grab, Gulp, Shower, Repeat

ELEPHANTS USE THEIR TRUNKS LIKE A HAND, NOSE, AND STRAW ALL IN ONE! THEY CAN USE THEM TO GRAB FOOD, DRINK WATER, AND EVEN GIVE THEMSELVES A SHOWER.

LONG LIVES

ELEPHANTS CAN LIVE A LONG TIME, UP TO 60 OR 70 YEARS, JUST LIKE PEOPLE.

GIANT EARS, BIG CHILL

ELEPHANTS' GIANT EARS AREN'T JUST FOR HEARING. THEY FLAP THEM TO STAY COOL, WORKING LIKE BUILT-IN FANS.

MANATEES

BIG & BEAUTIFUL

MANATEES ARE LARGE, WEIGHING BETWEEN 1,000 TO 1,300 POUNDS, AND THEY CAN GROW UP TO 13 FEET LONG!

Gentle Giants

MANATEES ARE BIG AND GENTLE! THEY'RE SOMETIMES CALLED "SEA COWS" BECAUSE THEY'RE SLOW AND LOVE TO GRAZE ON PLANTS.

BREATHING TIME

MANATEES CAN HOLD THEIR BREATH FOR ABOUT 15 TO 20 MINUTES WHEN THEY'RE RESTING. BUT WHEN THEY'RE ACTIVE, THEY COME UP FOR AIR EVERY FEW MINUTES.

Close Cousins to Elephants

MANATEES ARE RELATED TO ELEPHANTS! THEY EVEN HAVE TINY TOENAILS ON THEIR FLIPPERS, JUST LIKE ELEPHANTS HAVE ON THEIR FEET.

BADGERS

Nighttime Ninjas

BADGERS ARE NOCTURNAL, WHICH MEANS THEY COME OUT AT NIGHT TO HUNT FOR FOOD AND EXPLORE, WHILE SPENDING THE DAY SLEEPING IN THEIR DEN.

FAMILY TEAMS

BADGERS OFTEN LIVE IN GROUPS CALLED CLANS. THEY WORK TOGETHER TO DIG AND TAKE CARE OF EACH OTHER.

Bug and Berry Lovers

BADGERS ARE OMNIVORES, WHICH MEANS THEY EAT BOTH PLANTS AND ANIMALS. THEY ENJOY MUNCHING ON WORMS, INSECTS, BERRIES, AND EVEN SMALL MAMMALS.

FIERCE FIGHTERS

EVEN THOUGH BADGERS ARE SMALL, THEY'RE SUPER TOUGH AND BRAVE! THEY CAN DEFEND THEMSELVES AGAINST MUCH LARGER ANIMALS.

AXOLOTLS

THE SMILING SALAMANDER

AXOLOTLS ALWAYS LOOK LIKE THEY'RE SMILING BECAUSE OF THEIR CUTE, WIDE MOUTHS!

THEY NEVER GROW UP

AXOLOTLS STAY IN THEIR "BABY" FORM THEIR WHOLE LIVES, WHICH IS CALLED NEOTENY. THIS MEANS THEY KEEP THEIR GILLS AND LIVE IN WATER INSTEAD OF BECOMING LAND-DWELLERS.

TINY TEETH

AXOLOTLS HAVE TINY TEETH, BUT THEY DON'T CHEW THEIR FOOD. THEY SWALLOW IT WHOLE!

SUPER REGENERATORS

AXOLOTLS ARE LIKE SUPERHEROES! THEY CAN REGROW LOST BODY PARTS, INCLUDING LEGS, TAILS, AND EVEN PARTS OF THEIR HEARTS AND BRAINS!

CAMELS

Unique Walk

CAMELS HAVE A SPECIAL WAY OF WALKING. BOTH LEGS ON THE SAME SIDE MOVE TOGETHER, WHICH HELPS THEM STAY BALANCED ON SANDY GROUND.

Three Sets of Eyelids

TO PROTECT THEIR EYES FROM SAND AND DUST, CAMELS HAVE THREE SETS OF EYELIDS: TWO WITH LASHES AND ONE THIN, CLEAR EYELID LIKE GOGGLES.

WATER WIZARDS

CAMELS CAN DRINK UP TO 40 GALLONS OF WATER IN JUST ONE GO! THEY'RE GREAT AT STORING WATER IN THEIR BODIES TO STAY HYDRATED FOR DAYS.

PRICKLY EATERS

CAMELS CAN EAT THORNY PLANTS AND DRY GRASS THAT OTHER ANIMALS CAN'T. THEIR TOUGH MOUTHS HELP THEM CHEW WITHOUT GETTING HURT.

TIGERS

GREAT SWIMMERS

TIGERS LOVE WATER AND ARE FANTASTIC SWIMMERS. THEY OFTEN COOL OFF IN RIVERS AND LAKES AND CAN SWIM FOR MILES TO HUNT OR FIND NEW TERRITORY.

King of Big Cats

TIGERS ARE THE LARGEST WILD CATS ON EARTH. SOME CAN GROW UP TO 10 FEET LONG AND WEIGH OVER 600 POUNDS!

ROARING LOUD

A TIGER'S ROAR CAN BE HEARD FROM UP TO 2 MILES AWAY! THEY USE ROARS TO COMMUNICATE WITH OTHER TIGERS AND MARK THEIR TERRITORY.

Stripes as Unique as You!

EVERY TIGER HAS A UNIQUE PATTERN OF STRIPES, JUST LIKE YOUR FINGERPRINTS. NO TWO TIGERS HAVE THE SAME STRIPES!

NARWHALS

DEEP DIVERS

NARWHALS CAN DIVE SUPER DEEP—UP TO 5,000 FEET! THAT'S AS TALL AS TEN BIG SKYSCRAPERS STACKED ON TOP OF EACH OTHER.

TUSK MYSTERY

SCIENTISTS AREN'T TOTALLY SURE WHY NARWHALS HAVE TUSKS. SOME THINK THEY USE THEM TO IMPRESS OTHER NARWHALS, SHOW WHO'S IN CHARGE, OR EVEN BREAK ICE!

Arctic Experts

NARWHALS LIVE IN THE FREEZING ARCTIC WATERS NEAR GREENLAND, CANADA, AND RUSSIA, WHERE IT'S SUPER COLD ALL YEAR.

Unicorns of the Sea

NARWHALS HAVE A LONG, SPIRAL TUSK THAT LOOKS LIKE A UNICORN HORN! IT CAN GROW UP TO 10 FEET LONG AND IS ACTUALLY A BIG TOOTH.

FERRETS

NATURAL TUNNEL DIGGERS

FERRETS ARE EXCELLENT DIGGERS. THEY COME FROM A FAMILY OF ANIMALS THAT LOVE TO BURROW AND MAKE COZY TUNNELS UNDERGROUND.

TINY EXPLORERS

FERRETS ARE SUPER CURIOUS AND LOVE TO EXPLORE. THEY'LL CLIMB, SQUEEZE, AND WIGGLE THEIR WAY INTO SMALL SPACES TO SEE WHAT'S INSIDE!

SLEEPYHEADS

EVEN THOUGH THEY'RE PLAYFUL, FERRETS LOVE THEIR SLEEP. THEY CAN SNOOZE UP TO 18 HOURS A DAY TO RECHARGE.

Teeth for Treats

FERRETS HAVE SHARP TEETH, PERFECT FOR EATING MEAT. IN THE WILD, THEY HUNT SMALL ANIMALS LIKE RABBITS OR RODENTS.

APES

Gorilla Chest Beats

MALE GORILLAS BEAT THEIR CHESTS TO SHOW STRENGTH AND SCARE OFF RIVALS. IT'S LIKE THEIR VERSION OF SAYING, "I'M THE BOSS!"

SHARING IS CARING

BONOBOS ARE KNOWN FOR BEING GENTLE AND SOLVING PROBLEMS THROUGH COOPERATION AND SHARING INSTEAD OF FIGHTING.

AMAZING MEMORY

APES HAVE INCREDIBLE MEMORIES. THEY CAN REMEMBER LOCATIONS OF FOOD, FACES, AND EVEN PAST EVENTS.

Treetop Acrobats

GIBBONS ARE THE BEST SWINGERS IN THE APE FAMILY. THEY CAN TRAVEL UP TO 35 MILES PER HOUR THROUGH THE TREETOPS!

TOOL TIME

APES ARE CLEVER TOOL-USERS! CHIMPANZEES USE STICKS TO FISH FOR TERMITES, AND ORANGUTANS USE LEAVES AS UMBRELLAS OR TO DRINK WATER.

FAST LEARNERS

YOUNG APES LEARN BY WATCHING THEIR PARENTS. THEY PRACTICE SKILLS LIKE CLIMBING, FORAGING, AND EVEN PLAYING!

Closest Relatives to Humans

APES SHARE ABOUT 98% OF THEIR DNA WITH HUMANS! CHIMPANZEES AND BONOBOS ARE OUR CLOSEST ANIMAL RELATIVES.

NO TAILS AT ALL

UNLIKE MONKEYS, APES DON'T HAVE TAILS. INSTEAD, THEY HAVE STRONG LOWER BACKS AND HIPS THAT HELP THEM BALANCE AND CLIMB.

JUNGLE VEGGIE LOVERS

APES MAINLY EAT PLANTS LIKE FRUITS, LEAVES, STALKS, AND SEEDS, BUT THEY MAY ALSO EAT INSECTS OR SMALL ANIMALS

CAPYBARAS

PARTY ANIMALS

CAPYBARAS ARE VERY SOCIAL AND LIVE IN GROUPS OF 10 TO 20, BUT SOMETIMES AS MANY AS 100 CAPYBARAS CAN GATHER TOGETHER!

Rodent Royalty

CAPYBARAS ARE THE LARGEST RODENTS ON EARTH! THEY CAN GROW UP TO 4 FEET LONG AND WEIGH AS MUCH AS 150 POUNDS.

NATIVE TO SOUTH AMERICA

CAPYBARAS ARE FOUND IN SOUTH AMERICA, WHERE THEY LIVE IN FORESTS, GRASSLANDS, AND WETLANDS NEAR RIVERS AND LAKES.

SQUEAKY TALKERS

CAPYBARAS COMMUNICATE USING A VARIETY OF SOUNDS, LIKE WHISTLES, CLICKS, AND SQUEAKS. EACH SOUND HAS A DIFFERENT MEANING!

BISON

National Mammal of the U.S.

IN 2016, THE BISON WAS NAMED THE NATIONAL MAMMAL OF THE UNITED STATES BECAUSE OF ITS IMPORTANCE TO AMERICAN HISTORY AND CULTURE.

BISON OR BUFFALO?

PEOPLE OFTEN CALL THEM BUFFALO, BUT THEY'RE ACTUALLY BISON. TRUE BUFFALO LIVE IN AFRICA AND ASIA, LIKE THE WATER BUFFALO.

FAST RUNNERS

DESPITE THEIR SIZE, BISON ARE SURPRISINGLY FAST! THEY CAN RUN UP TO 35 MILES PER HOUR, FASTER THAN MOST PEOPLE CAN RIDE A BIKE.

The Great Comeback

BISON WERE ONCE NEARLY EXTINCT DUE TO OVERHUNTING, BUT CONSERVATION EFFORTS HAVE HELPED THEIR POPULATIONS GROW, AND NOW THEY ROAM FREE IN MANY NATIONAL PARKS!

CHEETAHS

Speed Demons

CHEETAHS ARE THE FASTEST ANIMALS ON LAND! THEY CAN RUN UP TO 70 MILES PER HOUR, BUT ONLY FOR SHORT DISTANCES.

CLAWS OUT

UNLIKE OTHER BIG CATS, CHEETAHS HAVE CLAWS THAT DON'T RETRACT, GIVING THEM EXTRA GRIP WHEN RUNNING AT HIGH SPEEDS.

QUIET CATS

UNLIKE LIONS AND TIGERS, CHEETAHS CAN'T ROAR. INSTEAD, THEY MAKE CHIRPING SOUNDS, PURRS, AND EVEN GROWLS TO COMMUNICATE.

MOHAWK MANE

CHEETAH CUBS ARE BORN WITH A FLUFFY MANE ALONG THEIR BACK THAT LOOKS LIKE A MOHAWK. IT HELPS THEM BLEND IN WITH TALL GRASS TO STAY SAFE FROM PREDATORS.

CHICKENS

RULES OF THE ROOST

CHICKENS LIVE IN GROUPS AND HAVE A SOCIAL HIERARCHY CALLED A "PECKING ORDER," WHERE SOME CHICKENS ARE MORE DOMINANT THAN OTHERS.

Chickens Can't Fly Far

CHICKENS CAN FLAP THEIR WINGS AND FLY SHORT DISTANCES, LIKE HOPPING OVER FENCES OR INTO LOW TREE BRANCHES, BUT THEY AREN'T GREAT FLYERS.

DIRT SPA

CHICKENS TAKE DUST BATHS TO KEEP CLEAN. THEY ROLL AROUND IN DIRT TO GET RID OF PESTS AND KEEP THEIR FEATHERS HEALTHY.

Egg-cellent Layers

ONE HEN CAN LAY AROUND 250 TO 300 EGGS IN A YEAR. THAT'S ALMOST ONE EGG EVERY SINGLE DAY! OF COURSE, HOW MANY EGGS SHE LAYS CAN DEPEND ON HER BREED, HOW OLD SHE IS, AND EVEN THE WEATHER.

OCTOPUSES

THREE HEARTS

OCTOPUSES HAVE THREE HEARTS! TWO PUMP BLOOD TO THEIR GILLS, AND THE THIRD PUMPS IT TO THE REST OF THEIR BODY.

Master of Disguise

OCTOPUSES CAN CHANGE THEIR SKIN COLOR AND TEXTURE TO BLEND IN WITH THEIR SURROUNDINGS. THIS HELPS THEM HIDE FROM PREDATORS OR SNEAK UP ON PREY.

No Bones About It

OCTOPUSES DON'T HAVE ANY BONES, WHICH MAKES THEM SUPER FLEXIBLE. THEY CAN SQUEEZE INTO TINY SPACES, EVEN AS SMALL AS A SODA BOTTLE!

EIGHT ARMS

OCTOPUSES HAVE EIGHT ARMS LINED WITH SUCTION CUPS THAT HELP THEM GRAB ONTO THINGS AND FEEL THEIR SURROUNDINGS. THAT'S WHY THEY'RE CALLED "OCTO," MEANING EIGHT!

HIPPOPOTAMUSES

VEGETARIAN GIANTS

HIPPOS ARE HERBIVORES, MEANING THEY ONLY EAT PLANTS. THEY LOVE TO MUNCH ON GRASS, EATING UP TO 80 POUNDS OF IT IN ONE NIGHT!

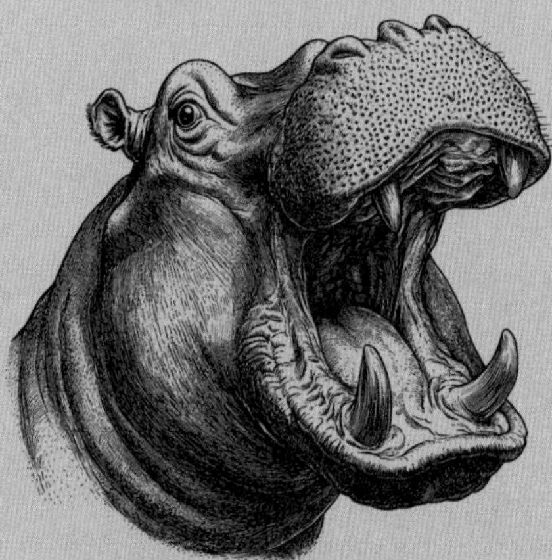

BIG MOUTHS

A HIPPO'S MOUTH CAN OPEN UP TO FOUR FEET WIDE. PERFECT FOR DEFENSE AND SHOWING OFF.

POD PALS

HIPPOS LIVE IN GROUPS CALLED PODS OR HERDS, USUALLY LED BY A DOMINANT MALE. A POD CAN HAVE UP TO 30 MEMBERS!

River Gliders

EVEN THOUGH THEY'RE HUGE, HIPPOS ARE GREAT SWIMMERS. THEY CAN EVEN WALK ALONG THE BOTTOM OF RIVERS AND PUSH THEMSELVES OFF TO GLIDE.

SNAILS

Slow and Steady

SNAILS ARE SOME OF THE SLOWEST CREATURES ON EARTH. THEY MOVE AT A SPEED OF ABOUT 0.03 MILES PER HOUR!

PORTABLE HOMES

SNAILS HAVE A HARD SHELL ON THEIR BACK THAT ACTS AS THEIR HOME. IF DANGER COMES, THEY CAN PULL THEIR WHOLE BODY INSIDE FOR PROTECTION!

SUPER SLEEPERS

SOME SNAILS CAN SLEEP FOR LONG PERIODS, EVEN UP TO THREE YEARS, WHEN THE WEATHER IS TOO DRY OR COLD.

Feel the Vibrations

SNAILS DON'T HAVE EARS, BUT THEY CAN SENSE VIBRATIONS TO DETECT DANGER OR MOVEMENT NEARBY.

COWS

HERD FRIENDS FOREVER

COWS ARE VERY SOCIAL AND FORM STRONG BONDS WITH OTHER COWS IN THEIR HERD. THEY EVEN HAVE BEST FRIENDS AND CAN FEEL LONELY WHEN SEPARATED.

MILK MAKERS

COWS PRODUCE MILK TO FEED THEIR CALVES, AND DAIRY COWS CAN PRODUCE UP TO 8 GALLONS OF MILK A DAY!

Moo-tastic Communicators

COWS "TALK" TO EACH OTHER BY MOOING. EACH MOO CAN HAVE A DIFFERENT MEANING, LIKE CALLING THEIR CALF OR ALERTING OTHERS ABOUT DANGER.

CHEW IT TWICE

COWS ARE RUMINANTS, WHICH MEANS THEY CHEW THEIR FOOD TWICE. THEY SWALLOW IT, BRING IT BACK UP AS CUD, AND CHEW IT AGAIN BEFORE FULLY DIGESTING IT.

PENGUINS

WADDLE WALKERS

PENGUINS HAVE SHORT LEGS AND WADDLE WHEN THEY WALK, WHICH MAKES THEM LOOK SUPER CUTE ON LAND.

EXCELLENT SWIMMERS

PENGUINS ARE AMAZING SWIMMERS! THEY CAN ZOOM THROUGH THE WATER AT SPEEDS UP TO 15 MILES PER HOUR USING THEIR FLIPPERS LIKE WINGS.

March of the Penguins

EMPEROR PENGUINS MARCH FOR MILES ACROSS THE ICE TO REACH THEIR BREEDING GROUNDS WHERE THEY LAY THEIR EGGS.

SHARED PARENTING

IN MANY PENGUIN SPECIES, BOTH MOM AND DAD TAKE TURNS KEEPING THE EGG WARM AND CARING FOR THEIR CHICK.

LIONS

The Loudest Roar

A LION'S ROAR CAN BE HEARD UP TO 5 MILES AWAY. THEY USE IT TO COMMUNICATE WITH THEIR PRIDE AND WARN OTHER LIONS TO STAY AWAY.

MANE EVENT

MALE LIONS HAVE THICK MANES, WHICH MAKE THEM LOOK BIGGER AND MORE INTIMIDATING TO RIVALS. THE DARKER THE MANE, THE HEALTHIER THE LION!

TEAM HUNTERS

LIONESSES ARE THE HUNTERS OF THE PRIDE, WORKING TOGETHER TO CATCH ANIMALS LIKE ZEBRAS, WILDEBEESTS, AND ANTELOPES.

Cubs Have Spots

LION CUBS ARE BORN WITH SPOTS ON THEIR FUR TO HELP THEM BLEND INTO THEIR SURROUNDINGS. THESE SPOTS FADE AS THEY GROW OLDER.

KANGAROOS

One Direction

KANGAROOS CAN'T WALK BACKWARD BECAUSE OF THE WAY THEIR LEGS AND TAIL ARE DESIGNED. THIS MAKES THEM A SYMBOL OF MOVING FORWARD IN AUSTRALIA!

JUMPING EXPERTS

KANGAROOS ARE AMAZING JUMPERS! THEY CAN LEAP UP TO 25 FEET IN A SINGLE JUMP AND TRAVEL AS FAST AS 35 MILES PER HOUR.

Big Feet, Big Hops

KANGAROOS HAVE STRONG HIND LEGS AND BIG FEET THAT HELP THEM HOP AROUND QUICKLY AND COVER LONG DISTANCES.

TAIL POWER

A KANGAROO'S TAIL IS LIKE A FIFTH LEG! THEY USE IT FOR BALANCE WHEN HOPPING AND AS SUPPORT WHEN STANDING.

ZEBRAS

Why Stripes?

ZEBRA STRIPES HELP THEM STAY COOL BY REFLECTING SUNLIGHT, CONFUSE PREDATORS, AND EVEN KEEP PESKY FLIES AWAY.

TALKATIVE TAILS

ZEBRAS USE SOUNDS LIKE BRAYING, BARKING, AND SNORTING TO COMMUNICATE. THEY ALSO USE BODY LANGUAGE, LIKE EAR MOVEMENTS AND TAIL SWISHING.

BUILT FOR TRAVEL

ZEBRAS MIGRATE LONG DISTANCES IN SEARCH OF FRESH GRASS AND WATER. THEY TRAVEL IN HERDS, SOMETIMES JOINING OTHER ANIMALS LIKE WILDEBEESTS.

THREE TYPES OF ZEBRAS

THERE ARE THREE MAIN TYPES OF ZEBRAS: PLAINS ZEBRAS, MOUNTAIN ZEBRAS, AND GREVY'S ZEBRAS. EACH TYPE LIVES IN DIFFERENT ENVIRONMENTS, FROM GRASSY PLAINS TO ROCKY HILLS.

INDEX